# For Better, For Worse

# For Better, For Worse

## *Sober Thoughts on Passionate Promises*

James Tunstead Burtchaell, C.S.C.

*Paulist Press* New York/Mahwah

Photographs used in this book are courtesy of Stephen Moriarty.

Portions of this book are adapted from the following publications, for which permission to republish here is gratefully acknowledged:

" 'Human Life' and Human Love," *Commonweal* 89,7 (15 November 1968): 245–252.

"Crises of Faith in Seminarians," *The Priest* 26,8 (September 1970): 9–19.

"In Loco Parentis: Life With(out) Father," *Notre Dame Magazine* 1,4 (August 1972): 20–23.

*Marriage Among Christians: A Curious Tradition* (Ave Maria, 1977).

"Christian Marriage: What's Good About It?" *Notre Dame Magazine* 7,2 (April 1978): 11–14.

"The Implausible Promise," *Notre Dame Magazine* 8,5 (December 1979): 26–29.

"Of Promises, Blood and Familial Bonds," *Parents* (Notre Dame Parents' Newsletter) 9,1 (Spring 1981): 1–2.

"Bonds of Promise, Bonds of Blood," *Respect Life!* (Bishops' Committee for Pro-Life Activities, 1983).

© 1985 by
James T. Burtchaell

Library of Congress
Catalog Card Number: 84-61489

ISBN: 0-8091-2664-8

Published by Paulist Press
997 Macarthur Boulevard
Mahwah, New Jersey 07430

Printed and bound in the
United States of America

# Contents

# *Introduction*

This book is written in order to pass on an understanding of marriage. It is a Christian tradition. It is not one that I can vouch for from my own personal experience, but that is not important. It is a tradition that I have learned about from many of its followers: most are long dead now, and some are very young today and finding that their experiences confirm the truth of this ancient wisdom.

There is wisdom in the Christian experience. Perhaps the fact that it has come under attack today should make us look at it more carefully.

Jesus surprised his followers by inviting them to a new kind of marital commitment: for better or for worse, until death. It was a frighteningly bold promise of fidelity, free of all conditions or escape-clauses, and so it asked for a more demanding love and a more secure trust. His followers found it a crazy sort of commitment, and he admitted it was, but said the Father made it possible, just as he made men and women able to set aside preferences to believe in and follow him.

This sort of commitment is terribly difficult to live up to, which is why more seasoned believers urge younger ones to approach it with caution. It is the decision of a lifetime, and one has to look past feelings of affection to find a deeper, firmer ground to rest it on.

There is a traditional wisdom about what are good grounds for marrying and what ones are unreliable. The first times together bring surprises, and it is no easy matter for two persons to become one household.

Ironically, one cannot count on marriage changing one's partner's shortcomings, but that is exactly what one hopes for from marriage.

Sex is meant to embody a surrender of privacy which comes from belonging to one another. It celebrates what marriage is, and is a deeper and more joyful experience for Christians who make these deeper promises. It is not simply an expression of love; rather, it embodies belonging— belonging in a way that only marriage quite achieves.

The love of marriage should welcome sharers, particularly children. The planning of birth is a reasonable thing, but there should be in the hearts of husbands and wives enough hunger and reverence for children that contraception would be used with thoughtfulness and reluctance, and abortion not even thought of.

Opportunities for women in society are multiplying, and our tradition needs to improve its understanding of how families grow when both parents, or just the wife-mother, will be active in careers. On this there is much learning to be done, but there are some cautionary things that should be shared with those who are beginning their journey on the road, to avoid anger and a sense that marriage stifles freedom.

Bad times are often good times in retrospect. The humor and patience and tolerance and sobriety which long marriages require can at least be suggested to the young.

The growth of marriage goes on and on and on. The adventures continue, and so do the challenges. There are times to grow when your children grow, and when they leave you, and when they have their own children, and when you are widowed. These experiences seem so far off to those approaching marriage, but should be at least glimpsed by them.

This congested account of our tradition is only a fraction of our inherited wisdom about marriage. Unfortunately, there are many young people who do not encounter even this much of it. Somehow their parents either disbelieved it or never took it in, and I see young folk marrying helter-skelter without even a suspicion of this awesome vision. They marry for better, not for worse. They speak of love, but it is something that happens to them, not something they do. Children are a burden to be indefinitely postponed. They couple in the teeth of clashing disagreements over basic values, and count on some future blending to bind them together, instead of confronting or even discussing their values beforehand. They mate when they are not mates, and seem never to have heard it convincingly said that sex means what marriage means—or that it means anything at all. They anticipate a future of a year or so, not of a lifetime.

## What Should You Get When You
## Give Yourself Away?

Because most of my work is as an educator, I deal
mostly with people going toward marriage. On the early
side of marriage, my overriding concern in counseling people is for them to acquire sober self-possession; their ability
to have in hand a person—themselves—whom they can
give away to someone else; their real capacity to make a
commitment that has any durability; their freedom from
artificial illusions about one another, about themselves and
about what marriage is all about. I find that I am speaking
out of the very center of the Catholic tradition of marital
fidelity. The strains that we naturally encounter when people live together in family are best understood if we realize
that we are all born selfish and must grow into love. There
is a very shrewd Christian conviction that to do this we
must dedicate ourselves to another person for life, and to
the children that issue from that commitment.

When are the motives for marriage worthy? I wish that
that were the question Christian men and women would
ask themselves. This is where older people can be of greatest service to young people, asking them the kind of testing,
probing questions that will allow young people to face
whether their intention has much freedom to it. Everyone
who wants to get married feels the same way. They all have
great determination, a great sense of affection for the other
person, a strong unflinching conviction that they are ready
to be married. Some of those people will move into won-
derfully mature marriages, and others within a matter of
years, months or even weeks will find that there was no
solidity to their intentions.

In civil law there is one type of undertaking that is always very subject to heavy scrutiny: wills that have been signed by very old or feeble people. The experience of society is that people can be coerced or, in other illegitimate ways, persuaded to dispose of their estates in ways they would not have done if they had been their younger, better selves. I suppose you could argue that people planning to marry are sometimes as little in possession of their right mind as feeble people being persuaded to sign away everything to a con man. Sometimes there is a good reason to inquire after-the-fact about whether people really were conscious and free in making this kind of choice. Some people who look as if they know what they're doing often have no sense of it at all. But more importantly: before-the-fact we ought to be more disturbed about the uncritical ease with which the Church is willing to celebrate frivolous marriages than we are about the quickness with which those marriages come to grief.

I think it's very rare that two people planning to marry are confronted by anyone who seriously asks them the tough questions that they would ask if they were going to do far less important things. Many parents would be more vocal about their children's decision to go into business or to sell a piece of property than about their decision to marry. And I think the clergy at this time are understandably but wrongly hesitant to look at a couple very closely and put the difficult questions to them.

Paradoxically, some of the most challenging questions have to be asked by couples who are least ready to question their relationship: those who have entered a sexual involvement or who have been living together. If sex needs to mean what marriage needs to mean, then a sexual exchange between a man and a woman who don't really belong to each other is doubly misleading. In one way, it is deceiving because they are saying things back and forth that are not true. The second thing is that a continual sexual bond between an unmarried man and woman inevitably arouses in them an artificially stimulated feeling that they really do belong to each other.

The Church invites people to give themselves away, on the belief that God makes such an apparently foolhardy thing possible and good. And the Church is wise in reminding us that sex has to do with children. It is clear that children are regarded as intruders in our society. A young woman I know recently sensed she was pregnant with what would be their third child. She called the local public health service to arrange a pregnancy test, and while she was on the telephone she was asked four times whether she "wanted to keep it." Her husband, who was teaching in a Catholic girls' high school, found that when he spread the news that they were going to have their third child, there wasn't a single person who responded with any kind of enthusiasm or congratulation. The people asked him, "Did it come as a surprise?" The most tactful way some could put it was, "Well, are you happy about it?" They found no one in their acquaintance, with the exception of a sister-in-law, who showed genuine happiness about the child.

A recent survey said that only fifty percent of men and women saw children as necessary to a good marriage. But the Christian tradition sees children as immensely important to a marriage. The dedication that it takes to see children through from infancy to adulthood is exactly the sort of burden that makes us grow up. Children make parents grow up a lot more than parents make children grow up.

There is a different kind of dedication required from a spouse than from a child. You are to be with your spouse through life. Your child is going to walk away from you. In one respect it requires more generosity to dedicate yourself to someone who will eventually leave you. Your child is by definition not very responsive, or thankful. Children seem to get adequately thankful just about the time when their parents die. I think there are all sorts of features to the love of children which cause personal maturity of a profound sort that even dedication to a spouse doesn't do.

We are all familiar with the social changes which have interfered with the conventional pattern: the man devoting all his energy to his career and the wife dedicating herself to the children. Many women now discover a very compelling desire to devote themselves wholly or partially to some sort of career or work. No one has shown it is possible for a husband and wife to be totally devoted to work outside the home throughout their married life and at the same time to rear children well. Therefore, a family can't have all of that at the same time. The trouble is that in the past whatever dedication to the children was necessary was thought to have to come from the mother. That was probably not very healthy, anyway. Pressure from the women's movement is going to provoke a welcome change among men who will have to reserve a more considerable portion of their energies for the family and children, especially during that very important time when children are young. Ironically, that is the time when most fathers feel the strongest need to compete in the professional world and to be absent from the home. What better time for the Church to be a voice that encourages young men and women to make a primary commitment to the goodness and maturity and health of their children, even in the teeth of professional competition?

So much attention can be paid to the way in which marriages fail that the real vision of what is good about Christian marriage often is lost. What is good about Christian marriage?

There is no other human bond that gives us quite this hope that the Father of Jesus is as we believe he is: relentlessly and stubbornly devoted to us. The ability of Christians to sustain faithful marriage throughout a lifetime is our strongest and most defiant assertion that the world is a crazy place and really makes good sense only to those who believe in mad things like Jesus being the Son of God, dying for those who killed him, or people willing to suffer for the sake of truth or their faith, and people willing to forfeit their own convenience throughout the span of a lifetime in order to make a common household with someone. And if Christians can go through a lifetime without doing things of that defiant sort, then I don't think we have any gumption or joy to show for our faith.

Tradition is not something one merely receives from one's elders and is expected to abide by. Every generation must put a tradition to the test, and must have its turn at reframing it. No tradition can be handed on with benefit unless one's predecessors can vouch that it has proved true in their own experience. So it cannot be imposed: only offered. As one who has listened to many married people I pass on here their insights to others. Those who receive it must submit the tradition to their own reflections and trials. It will bring good questions before them as they make their own journey across life, and it will remind them in their turn to pass on the wisdom as they would state it, lest their children be left empty-handed when their own hands had been filled, so to speak, as they were leaving home.

# 1     *For Better, For Worse*

Many new formats for marriage are being suggested and tried out these days. Some seem peculiar. One of the oddest sorts of marriage (thought not very new) continues to be the Christian kind customary among Catholics. I am going to try to show the sense underneath this Christian tradition. It is not exclusive to Catholics, and they are not always faithful to it, but it is in that denomination that this Christian tradition has best survived.

At the outset one thing needs to be said clearly: Catholics do not believe that there is only one way for people to marry—our way—nor do they insist that other arrangements should be forbidden. Quite the contrary: our particular custom of marriage is so strange that one could not expect it to make much sense to those outside our Christian household. Only within the context of a peculiar faith would such marriage not seem strange. Our matrimony promises just about the same things that our baptism does. People who think that this bunch of Christians are generally sensible and sober about their religion but a little peculiar in their views on matrimony are wrong. We are crazy in every way.

If in a certain society a woman is permitted to have six husbands, then the Church has no right and no desire to tell her that she only *thinks* she has six, whereas in reality one is the limit and five must go. If a man desires to acquire spouses by the half-dozen, the state may call him an outlaw; but if the state allows it, then our Church must simply acknowledge that he has six wives (though we believe that, in the matter of spouses, less is more). If in a certain culture it is accepted that men and women marry only for as long as they wish and can then be free to remarry others: well, we refrain from muttering that this is only licensed promiscuity. If people set out to marry, then they are married. Marriage is what one makes it—or what two make it. And society has developed a number of ways of doing it. We can think our way more promising without claiming that all other ways are illegitimate.

One hears the complaint that the Church is too legalistic on issues of marriage and divorce, and that it ought to reform its legislation in the way that most countries have. But it is the state, not the Church, which asserts its right to govern marriage and divorce by law. The state insists on its right to license (and in some countries to witness) marriages, and to grant divorces on its terms.

By contrast with the state, and with what many think, the Church has no comparable list of laws controlling marriage and forbidding divorce. The regulations which do exist bind the clergy more than those who propose to marry or unmarry. Admittedly there is a lot of activity in our chanceries and curia that gives off the sound and smell of legalism. Sometimes, unfortunately, the Church tries to bully a country into recognizing only the Catholic usage of marriage (previously the case in Italy, no better than the present laws in Israel which oblige all Jews to observe Orthodox Jewish usages). But no Christian church should claim any more than the right all citizens have to use the political process to press for marriage laws which seem best to them. Still, the legalistic business in church precincts does not involve clergy telling laity how and where and if they may marry. It involves, instead, churchmen determining for themselves when they may celebrate marriages truthfully and in adequate consistency with both faith and good sense. As a priest, I cannot with full conscience and exuberance officiate at a marriage which seems to be folly from the start. If I decline to do so, I am not telling a couple they cannot marry; I am saying that I cannot see how I can stand at the head of the Christian congregation and lead them in this celebration. Actually, rather than being less finicky about who is married, we probably should be more finicky about who is baptized and who is ordained.

The point is that the Church does not control or govern marriage. It *preaches* marriage: a particular sort of marriage in a particular sort of spirit. It celebrates marriage, though only its own kind. It encourages people to give their whole hearts to one another in marriage. It supports those who have tried to do so. And it grieves for those who suffer in or abandon their marriages. But unlike the state it does not and cannot force people to practice what it preaches. Its business is to celebrate, rather than to legislate.

But doesn't the Church have laws forbidding divorce? No, it does not. The Church since Paul has insisted that there is one bond more basic than marriage: the bond of faith. If the two bonds get tangled up, it is the bond of marriage which can be undone to unsnarl the bond of faith. But when confronted with a marriage that is in and of the faith, the Church has no laws on divorce. Instead, it confesses its incompetence to devise any law that could dissolve oaths made to be indissoluble. It claims to lack authority to declare its marriages finished and to celebrate new ones atop the ruins of the old. No one has ever sensibly explained how these promises, freely and knowingly made, "for better, for worse, until death," could truthfully and effectively be made to another person before death, no matter how bad the "worse" had become. The Church believes it can invite its members to enter some undertakings which are beyond its own power to govern.

Part of today's confusion regarding matrimony comes from the fact that so many wedding rituals deceive. Unfortunately most states in the Western world, and also many Christian denominations, use marriage rituals that are descended and adapted from the old Catholic rites. Not adapted enough, perhaps. Through one formula or another, men and women are led by judges and ministers into promises they may not really mean. They are being made to say that they bind themselves solemnly by oath to one another for life. Yet neither the state nor their church nor their society nor the couple has this understanding of what is being promised.

What is really meant is that the man and woman will remain as husband and wife as long as they want to, and that they *expect,* but do not *pledge,* that their union will last until death. If these promises were worded according to what people mean, people might be less deceived. In fact, most marriage rituals should probably leave out promises, pledges, or oaths. So many couples do not *do* something at their wedding; they announce that something *has happened* to them. They think their marriage is a public declaration of a joyful compatibility they hope will last; they do not commit themselves to one another irrevocably, believing that there will be seasons when both joy and compatibility seem lost in the fog and clouds, and promising that even then they will sail on.

If the state and many churches rewrote their marriage rituals to conform to what they really expect of brides and grooms, two things would follow. There would be less ungrounded romanticism at the time of marriage and there would be less sadness at the time of divorce. And we would see fewer things like trial marriages, pre-nuptial property agreements, contract cohabitation, etc. No need for this kind of hedging, when marriage itself has nothing irrevocable about it.

Let every tradition, every society, every church and every state—even every man and woman—make such marriages if they want to. The Christians I speak of ask only the freedom to offer their children a kind of promising that is more promising, a kind of undertaking that is more dreadful, a kind of joy that is firmer grounded. We do not claim to prevent failure, either by assuring spouses that they will always live up to their promises or by making the promises so weak that nothing is ventured and nothing gained. The Church does, however, claim that the most miserable failure can be swallowed up in forgiveness. It even hints that the most exquisite kinds of success grow in the soil of failure. The Church has no right to condemn other traditions and ventures, but it notices that many accommodations made to human failure seem to make the worst kinds of failure more likely.

But I must acknowledge what every reader has already noticed: that this vision of marriage, while native to the mind of the Church, is not at home in the mind of every communicant. It has taken distorted forms at times, and harsh tones that were not in Jesus' message. We owe it a better and more faithful presentation.

It would be senseless for Catholics to urge on others our vision of marriage if they do not share our vision of Jesus and the faith. We should try to understand both better ourselves, and to live both better—and then to explain how we see faith in the Father of Jesus and faithfulness to a sworn spouse as similarly possible, and similarly demanding, and similarly hazardous.

## Jesus Breaks with Tradition

It has been believed by Catholics that, because of Jesus, Christians developed a new way of marrying. Scattered through the Gospel are traces of the two basic sayings of Jesus on the subject: "What God has united, man must not divide" (Mk 10:9, Mt 19:6), and "The man who divorces his wife and marries another is guilty of adultery against her" (Mk 10:11; Mt 19:9; Lk 16:18).

The sense of Jesus' teaching shows clearest in Matthew's nineteenth chapter. The chapter presents two scenarios, told side-by-side. In one of the two stories Jesus is approached by a young man who obviously intends to find out more about the traveling rabbi and his program. He asks a standard leading question: "Master, what good deed must I do to possess eternal life?" Jesus' answer is, to start with, a standard one. He cites some of the more familiar commandments about not giving perjured evidence, not killing, not committing adultery, and so on. The young man warms to this teaching, for he claims to have kept these commandments since childhood. Is there anything else to be done? Indeed there is. Jesus goes on to say that if he wishes to complete the task he must sell all his possessions, give the proceeds to the poor, and join Jesus in his wanderings. At this the young man's smile fades, and instead of joining Jesus' followers, he disappears in the opposite direction. The writer tells us that he would have had a large estate to liquidate.

The disciples, who had not had long to think about having a rich man (even a formerly rich man) in their group, seem to have wondered whether a more discreet response by Jesus might have kept the young recruit from being frightened away. But Jesus takes them aside and makes his meaning even stiffer: it would be easier to thread a needle with a camel than for a rich man to possess eternal life. There is no mistaking his message now, and in dismay they comment that this is mad: on these terms no one would ever make the attempt. Yes, says Jesus: now they begin to glimpse the point. It is indeed crazy, but God can and will give people the strength to do it. Then, in case they imagine that he is only speaking about wealth, he tells them that a person must leave behind kin, property and land to wander with him. They must, in a word, quit home with its security and go wandering about after him among the world's strangers, on the prowl for those in need.

Jesus, in Matthew's Gospel, repeatedly confronts the religion of his time and place in ways that would have applied as well to religions of other times, places, and peoples. He directs his criticism toward what the Jews treasured as a most valuable benefit from God: the law. A Jew felt that the law was a relief, not a burden. Unlike other peoples, the Jews had been told—and in some detail—what it was God expected of them. To come before the living God one day was dreadful enough; far worse and more terrifying to do so without a hint of what terms one would be judged on. The more explicit the law, then, the greater a gift it became.

When a young man became an adult he accepted his divinely specified obligations. He entered life with open eyes; he knew what he was undertaking. But this undertaking was, according to Jesus, insufficient. The Father's claims were limitless, as was his love. No laws could contain them. From men and women he required an endless service, an open-ended dedication. At no point could one say that one had satisfied God's claim on one; at the end everyone would have to wring one's hands and admit that one was an unprofitable servant. No, God's claims were measured, not by a specified set of commandments or duties, but by the limitless misery and need of all fellow humans and by the limitless love which Jesus himself brought to this want. Jesus called on his followers to move beyond a religion of laws, to a religion of dedication to persons and their service.

Jesus' call beckoned people in the same direction as the law had drawn them, but he provoked them to journey even farther on that path. This did not mean that behavior forbidden under the old laws now became acceptable. On the contrary, the new commandment was much more strict, since one could never know in advance just what one's service would have to be, or how much would be required of one. By choosing to follow Jesus in his least brothers and sisters one was walking into the unknown. There would be many who, like the young man, preferred to do it by commandments, rather than put their whole heart and strength into his service. Their reach, sadly, would not extend quite far enough to put eternal life within their grasp.

Now the other story in Matthew 19 is a twin of that one. Jesus is approached by a group of devout religious types who want to know where he stands in a contemporary religious controversy. Some rabbis had held that adultery was the only legitimate ground for divorce; others were allowing that lesser offenses would justify it. Where did Jesus stand: with the conservatives or with the liberals? With neither. He stormed at them that divorce for any reason was evil in God's sight, and had only been a concession by Moses to the mean spirits of the people. (Do not be misled by the exception, "except for unchastity," Matthew's reference to the divorces that the Church of his time was imposing on convert couples when the spouses were close relatives. Roman custom allowed cousins and even siblings to marry; Jewish custom had considered such unions "unchaste," and Christians abided by this Jewish view.)

Here too Jesus' disciples, as startled as his questioners, draw him aside and suggest that he has possibly overstated his point, that he really must have meant to be more tactful and moderate than he sounded. Not at all. Jesus makes his point even clearer. If a man is betrayed by his wife and abandoned, and as a result suffers the worst imaginable misfortune—being left childless, no better than a eunuch— even then he should stand fast and faithful and count himself happy in the kingdom. (At this point, lest his readers think that Jesus is down on children, Matthew introduces the playground scene where Jesus welcomes the youngsters ignored by the disciples.) This is crazy, his disciples warn, and impossible besides. Few would risk a marriage that

allowed of no escape. Insane, yes; impossible, no, replies
Jesus. It is, again, one of those crazy things God can make
the human heart capable of.

When a young Jew married, the limits of his or her
undertaking were known in advance. The acceptable
grounds for divorce, after all, helped illustrate their commitment. They entered with open eyes. They knew what
their obligations would be, for they were revealed to them
from the start. But Jesus, in repudiating divorce, is pro-
moting a radically different sort of marriage. One would
bind oneself to a person, not to a specific set of conditions
or duties. One's duties would be measured, not by limits
calculated in advance, but by another person's needs: needs
which can never quite be calculated beforehand, needs
which seem never to be met. Jesus calls men and women
to a union that is frightening because the legitimate claims
on one's generosity are open-ended.

What happens at baptism is much the same as what
happens in matrimony. Both religion and marriage are
transformed, and both similarly: each had been determined
by law; now each will be determined by human need and
by divine generosity. Each had required obedience. Now
that will not go far enough, and love—love without limits—will be the most essential virtue. Put another way: obedience is still required, but now the partners must obey new
commands revealed in the unwritten law of their neighbor's (and each other's) need. Some participants will be
called to render astonishingly sacrificial service, far beyond
their imagining or their present strength. Both commitments—baptism and marriage—will summon forth fathomless faith, if one is to have enough trust to follow

another pledge-partner—spouse or Lord—wherever that might lead.

Matthew was not implying that all Jewish understanding of the law was grudging and narrow. There had always been prophets and sages who called their fellow Jews beyond a literal observance. What alarmed Matthew was a tendency already as evident in the young Christian community as it had been in Israel: to tame God's call by defining and limiting it. When he portrays Jesus as ignoring the law and inviting disciples to an unlimited neighbor-service, or ignoring divorce and inviting spouses to an unlimited fidelity, it is at Christians, not Jews, that he is aiming his story. In his day and in our day, followers of Jesus have flinched at his teaching that if we cannot keep faith with one another we cannot be faithful to him. To be steadfast to the Lord who cherishes us when we fail him requires no less than that we maintain fidelity to one another, for better or for worse.

A marriage that can be dissolved is a marriage of hedged love, just as a religion that can be satisfied by obedience to a set law is a religion of hedged love. Jesus invites men and women, without contracts or conditions, to make reckless promises to one another. And so, not knowing what lies before them, they promise to be true to one another, for better, for worse, for richer, for poorer, in sickness and in health, until death. Crazy. But no more so than that other oath to love the Lord with their whole heart and soul and strength, and to love one another as he has loved them.

What is extraordinary about these promises is not that they will summon up a gutsy determination to survive the crises when they rise up in anyone's married life. The difference shows itself at the very threshold of life together. It affects the promises made at marriage time, and the way they are kept from that day on. A man and woman pledge themselves, not to joy or to peace or to satisfaction, but to fidelity, from which joy and peace and satisfaction are believed to spring. They do not proclaim their delight and then hope that it will carry them through duty. They celebrate duty and accept what delight that will bring. The bond is absolutely different from every other marriage bond—from the outset.

## Pledging

At this point something should be said about pledging. It is the ancient observation of nearly everyone that humans arrive in life caring about themselves, and that they are all too likely to remain that way. It is the ancient belief of Christians that, with God's help and others' too, we can grow from self-centeredness into love—and that we urgently need to do so. One of the most powerful ways to emerge from egotism into love is pledging. To pledge is to put oneself at another's service, to give someone a *claim* upon oneself.

Pledge yourself to another and you are doubly bound. You now must be of service, no matter how you or your life or your partner should change. Secondly, the measure of your giving must be not what you would like to give, but what the other person needs. It is no longer a matter of doing good for someone. You give another person a claim upon yourself: what the other person claims, depending upon his or her developing needs, lies beyond your control.

There are some surprises, disappointments, and sacrifices; ironically you can know they are bound to come, but when they do come they have strange names and unfamiliar faces. A pledged person, in short, is repeatedly called to love more than he or she had planned, or perhaps even wished.

Pledging is a yielding of choice, a mortgaging of say-so over one's own affairs. But it is really an obligation that is liberating. Precisely by rising to meet one's commitments a person grows to have a greater and more giving will. There is always the fear that, after pledges are made, one will see the other person change. The affection and trust may then dissolve, leaving one bound to carry out commitments joy-lessly or alone. Those who are held back by this fear imag-ine that it is attraction to another which supports fidelity and makes it joyful. The reverse is more often true. It is in keeping our pledges to people that we both notice and invite them to be even more attractive than we had first seen or they had first been. Affection is a weak and fickle foundation for service. Service, though, is the best footing that affection is ever likely to have.

Christian marriage is the most awesome pledge one human being can give to another: for better, for worse, until death. In fact, the only pledge like it is the faith we pledge to the Lord or, better still, the faith the Lord pledges to us. In both cases we attempt to respond to and reproduce in ourselves the fidelity pledged to us by God who is Fidelity himself. Between man and wife it is as between disciple and Jesus: one will be loved, one can claim to be loved, what-ever one's faults. One need not worry whether one will con-tinue to be cherished. One is always forgiven before the fall.

Making pledges and keeping them are not the same thing. Sacrifice of our convenience to another's need, after all, rubs against the grain. But we have to remember that the strength to make good on these promises is itself promised. And whoever lives faithfully and generously in marriage need not fear that he or she will default on larger claims. There are none larger.

Perhaps this is why thoughtful Catholics persist in their curious tradition despite the obvious warning that leaving oneself so entirely at the mercy of another is a mighty risk and may be steering into bitter sorrow. But all Christian sacramental pledges are taken facing Jesus crucified, and no pledge can lead us around suffering. No pledge is great if it does not somehow pass us through fire and sorrow. Pledged marriage is a little like childbirth. Afterward everyone tells you how marvelous it was, but it took a lot of pain and struggle to get to that point.

The Christian tradition doubts that a person will come to full human maturity or possess eternal life without some pledging to other people: for better, for worse, until death. The young man in Matthew's story had the disadvantage of being rich: the sort of fellow who could easily lay claims on others, while evading theirs on him. Wealth, though, is only one way to evade claims. We are stubbornly selfish creatures. We are not likely to grow unless committed. To pledge without evasion is to expose ourselves to risk—but not to any risk that was not already there. For what it takes to serve our pledge-partners when they are moody and ungrateful and mean and infuriating is exactly what it takes if we are to grow up. It is difficult to serve anyone; more difficult when the terms of service are unspecified; and most difficult when there is no end to the service. Only one thing in the world is more difficult: to serve only those we like, to the extent that it is agreeable, and for as long as we please. This is not just difficult; it is truly impossible. We end up serving no one but ourselves. That is why we have to pledge.

## Courting for Keeps

If Christian marriage binds you for life, for better or for worse, then courtship is one of the most crucial times in your life. You are faced with the most important of choices, and the wisdom or the stupidity of the choice will cling to your soul for life—in fact, it is one of those decisions whose outcome reaches beyond death.

The crisis, however, is not so much how to choose the right person as how to marry the person you chose. I have often had the impression, when homes and hearts are broken by divorce, that the cause of hostility and separation was not the unsuitability of the parties for one another. In fact, it is very difficult to discover basic marital "incompatibilities" which are beyond anyone's control; they tend to be very ordinary human faults that no one wishes to control. The cause of failure seemed to be that the couple had not really given themselves away to each other. If this hunch is correct, then whom one marries is less important than how. But one of the best ways to find out the kind of marriage you are headed for is to look at the kind of person you wish to marry and try to understand what draws you together.

Let me try to use a few ordinary examples to illustrate how marriages wither. Boy marries girl because of her slim figure, and only later discovers that her wits are similarly slender. Girl has been too long stifled at home, and will marry anyone who wants to emancipate her. Boy marries pregnant girl (who decided to get pregnant) because then she and their parents will no longer hold him guilty. Girl marries boy who has apparently walked away from a tragic marriage in which he was misunderstood and misappreciated. (I would apologize for these melodramatic examples if they happened less often.) What is the disaster? In these circumstances it is very easy to marry the wrong person. It is extremely difficult, in fact, to marry a right person. This doesn't necessarily mean, however, that a decent person has mistakenly married a rotten one. People usually get what they deserve in marriage. Most anyone who marries the wrong person is himself or herself also the wrong person. More to the point: the marriage is wrong, often wrong from the start, and made wrong by two persons who, whatever their faults, might have married well—even to the same partners.

Is the bond between a couple generous or selfish? Granted that in almost all courtships there is and should be a pleasure and a passion and much fun, the soundness of any prospective marriage has to be estimated by how prepared the man and woman are to sacrifice their own preferences for one another without brooding over it. This is a difficult judgment to make, and most difficult for those who have the most at stake. The most critical judgment of a lifetime has to be made before enough lifetime has passed by to make one very critical in judging. The most frivolous courtships and the most wonderful courtships generally feel the same to their chief participants. How are the parties facing engagement supposed to form a sensible judgment about themselves?

No one seems to ask parents or grandparents anymore. I suspect it is not so much the young who don't want to ask as it is their elders who don't quite know how to answer. Once upon a time our society required folks to stay married, and parents told their children whom to marry. Time passed, and there followed a period when society still expected you to stay married, but you were left free to choose your own spouse. Today, after further change, society leaves you free to decide whom to marry, and similarly free to keep your promises or not. This, we are told, is social progress.

The ideal parents are supposed to be wise enough not to impose their own judgment on the youngsters. But I wonder how fair it is for young people bent on marriage not to have tough questions, welcome or not, put to them by their elders. What can older people offer? If they have at least some good sense and enough affection and respect for the young people, they will not be able to tell anyone whom to marry, but they can say what, if anything, they find faulty in the match that is in the making. A person's parents or shrewd friends might not always be right about the character of a fiancé or a fiancée but they might have important things to say about how their own child or friend shows character in the companionship.

The tradition offers a few wise words to those who want to test their own desire to marry. One concerns time. A wise engagement will generally take a long period of companionship beforehand. And the companionship should involve all sorts of circumstances, not just social amusement. If you are antagonized by your friend's family, find her friends a bit disagreeable, his taste crude, her conversation waning after the first quarter-hour, his interests warming most to things that leave you cold—but are willing to overlook all that because you love him or her so very much and will be able in time to change all that . . . well, you are canoeing toward the falls. But if you don't even allow the kind of time and situations required to know family and friends and tastes and mind, to let boredom or vexation or picky-picky selfishness come to the surface . . . you are heading for the brink, with your eyes closed.

A second cue from the tradition is that sex is usually a disastrous prelude to marriage. Sexual union needs to mean personal union, and if a man and woman have not merged their two lives into one, sex does not tell the truth. Worse, it is so powerful an experience that a continued sexual relationship arouses in a couple the feelings of being one, even though they are still very much two. The feelings are artificially produced but, like all things counterfeit, they feel like the real thing, especially to those who have never felt the real thing. I can hardly think of a way for two people better to conceal from themselves their true relationship and prospects for marriage than becoming sexually involved. And there is no time in their lives when reliable self-evaluation is more crucial.

## Sex

Sex, they say, is a subject upon which Holy Mother Church has been a real scold. Whatever the failings of her spokesmen, the Church's fundamental understanding of sex has been strongly positive. When you believe that sex both requires and confers exquisite love and fidelity, you become annoyed at seeing it frivolously understood and frivolously used. The Declaration of Independence is a carping and complaining document, but that is because the founding fathers were high on freedom and had seen too little of it. Conservationists tend to come across to the public as quarrelsome because there are woodlands and waterways they know are precious but which are squandered and abused. There is always unpleasant talk from people who value something highly and mean to see it protected from debasement.

The Church has two fairly simple teachings about sex. The first is that sex is supposed to mean what marriage is supposed to mean. The second is that sex reveals meaning, but cannot produce it.

The belief that sex is an expression of love is widespread and well received. Our tradition says otherwise. Not that one shouldn't and doesn't convey love sexually. But love is not what makes the sexual exchange truthful; and love alone cannot prevent its spoilage. There are, after all, countless acts of love: carrying in the groceries, embracing, or offering one's kidney for a transplant. None of these need be sexual. There may be many people whom one loves profoundly, yet without sexual expression. Sex is not the only expression of love, nor the necessary one. It is not even the greatest: you love your parents as deeply as anyone but you do not have sex with them; that does not mean that you love them less than you love your spouse. It does mean that your love for them is specifically different. Sex is appropriate, not simply to exquisite love, but to a very special kind: pledged love, faithful love, fidelity.

What is truthful, proper, distinctive, and defining about sexual union is that it means: "I take you, for better, for worse, until death." It means belonging. Of course it is

meant to be an expression of love. You will never live up
to it without love. But it is not love which gives it truth. It
must embody the love between two persons who can say to
one another, and to no other living person: "I am yours,
and all that I have is yours. All that each of us has is not
'mine' or 'yours' but 'ours.'" This is a love-pledge you do
not make even to your children. You may not love them
less, but you love them differently.

The sharing of the body's privacy is, or ought to be, the
sharing of the person's privacy. Only to a spouse has one
truly yielded one's privacy—that which is "mine and no
one else's," in person and property. And only with a spouse
can sex grow to good maturity.

Believing as they do that a couple can and should
pledge themselves without reserve or condition, Catholics
naturally consider sex a more joyful exchange, because it
can have so much more to convey. Believing that it can
celebrate an almost unbelievable fidelity, Catholics also
naturally see greater loss and greater confusion when sex is
used for other, lesser purposes. This, I suppose, is what has
brought on all the cautionary talk.

Someone has said that sex will make a good relationship better, but cannot make a bad one good. This leads to
the second point about sex: it is not a source of meaning,
but a celebration of it. If the meaning is there, there is
hardly a better way to celebrate it. When meaning is not
there, a counterfeit is put in its place that makes the truth
harder to restore.

A couple makes love by the tens of thousands of ges-
tures of generous, cheerful, humorous, or even dogged ser-

vice toward one another or family. Love is made by remembering to put anti-freeze in the car, by not insisting that one's spouse listen to positively everything that happened since breakfast, by not drinking too much, and by taking the children to the zoo and smacking the one who fed copper pennies to the seals despite the sign on the wall. So it goes. This how to *make* love. Couples who do care for one another in this fashion celebrate this sexually and enjoy and are grateful for the profound personal affection sheltered within such workaday services. If there are failures in these personal bonds of fidelity—and there are always failures—a couple's sexual exchange may reveal them or distract from them, but by itself it cannot reverse them, nor can it be quite right itself until they are corrected.

Sex cannot give truth to a couple's life together. But neither can it destroy it. Much of the sex research and therapy and counseling done today seems to assume that households are strained to the breaking point by sexual malfunction or ineptitude. Anyone can have sexual difficulties and I suppose that most can be helped out of them. So much the better. But this kind of problem is not at all of the same order or magnitude, say, as alcoholism. The one problem can be borne if other features of the relationship are sound; the other can put the rot into every feature of the relationship. Any couple which imagines its major frustrations and antagonisms come from sexual clumsiness has a real problem, but it isn't sexual.

Sex is like marriage, and both are like life. People take their life to bed with them. But you can enjoy sex or marriage or life with gusto only if you ground yourselves on commitments that are true and trusted.

## Childbearing

Taking children into one's life is a part of good marriage. It is also part of good sex—and of good life. Some say you are never really married until children have arrived. Without going even that far one could say that you are never really married if you have had no appetite for children. If that be true, there are many couples who are not really married—and many couples with children who are not really married.

Many couples do not crave children. This is not because they know we face an overpopulation problem. No matter how aware they are of this problem (and it is a grave problem), men and women make their childbearing decisions from motives more personal, more close to home. Those who tend to act on population worry are wealthy people (and nations) who plead with or pay or sterilize poor people (and nations) not to have so many children because they, the wealthy, think there are things ever so much more important than children, and, besides sharing this insight with the poor, would just as soon not have so many poor kids to pay for. If they really were supporting the children of the poor their birth control programs would probably work better.

Couples shirk children, naturally enough, because children are a burden. A child, unlike a spouse, has to be taken into one's life without one's being able to choose his or her personality. A child claims one's heart and drains one's substance, and then grows up and goes away, without your being sure the child will bring you pride or chagrin. Most obviously, a child costs cash and comfort and convenience.

Children are a burden. A spouse, though, is a burden too. There is a difference: one's partner never seems a burden in the beginning; the bleakness shows later. But one's children can seem a burden even before they come. The challenge and the duty and the grace in both is that one be made to grow to love him/her/them so much that serving is no longer burdensome.

Most couples who marry today do not actually refuse children. But many postpone them indefinitely. By "indefinitely" I do not mean that they await the moment when finances and location and careers will make a child feasible, though at the moment they can't quite anticipate when that will be. The indefiniteness often means that conditions are not yet ripe for a child, and the couple really has no clear idea when they will be ripe, or what ripe conditions they are waiting for. They simply don't welcome children yet, and they are waiting to want them. They "need time to get to know one another." Eventually they will probably have to make a decision to have a child. Some people think it healthier that children come from such clear decisions. The tradition said that, when children come, they should come from the original decision to marry, for marriage and child-bearing were a single summons and a single joy. If, by the time a couple finally consent to have a child, the generosity and openness of their marital decision are waning, and there is a fixed and comfortable round of life into which another comes as an intruder—well, is that healthier?

Children are part of marriage, and husband and wife mean household and family. One does have a different love affair with one's children. Out of the sharing of deepest privacy come sons and daughters who share all but that privacy. They need to be given enough privacy and self to take away with them what they will later be able to give away to another. It cannot be very easy to devote oneself heart and soul to a person, and then see that person turn away to become devoted to a stranger. Or to give children gifts which are better than they can then appreciate, which will probably be forgotten by the time they've grown enough to appreciate and thank you for them. The most generous things you can do are done for children who are still growing, and who will therefore probably take those gifts for granted. One has to love very much to raise children, which is why they are good for people.

It tends to make one less selfish to beget and bless and liberate children. Parents who do it well tell me that doing it side-by-side is the best way for a husband and wife to get to know one another and appreciate one another.

What is wanted is neither "every family a Trapp Family" with 12+ children filling the happy, boisterous household (it may likely be more boisterous than happy), nor every home producing 2.2 children according to calculated growth needs issued by the Secretary of the Interior. Far better for young couples to crave a child and, having been gifted and grown a bit with it, to make their decision about another on the strength of what they are learning. To calculate how many children you will have before ever holding your own baby in your hands is not very wise.

Some years back Pope Paul published a letter on birth control which missed the mark. He was trying to argue, to a world unwelcoming to children, that marriage and sex were wrong and selfishly perverted if intentionally closed to childbearing. He was arguing as the tradition argues, but not as well. He taught that every single act of sexual intercourse had to be free of any humanly contrived interference with conception, but he did allow that the sequence of intercourse could be harmonized with the rhythm of the monthly fertility cycle so that conception would be unlikely. He called rhythm "natural" and other contraception "artificial." His argument might have been more faithful to the tradition, more persuasive, and less disastrous for the Church had he turned it around. It matters less whether any single act of sex be open to conception than whether the entire sequence (not of a month but of a lifetime) of giving and sex and marriage be open to family. Let a couple determine how they will welcome their children, provided they have a welcome for children.

## A Crazy Idea in the First Place

These are a few thoughts about what a man and woman face together if they take one another, for better, for worse, for richer, for poorer, in sickness and in health, until death do them part. If they do it with good and giving hearts, and grow to give more and more, they will sometimes hurt but never be confounded. It is, as Jesus admitted, crazy. But we have faith that if a person have love enough to lay down his or her life for a friend and spouse in marriage, they will both share a kind and quality of love and life which perhaps not even death can part.

# 2 *How to Decide on Marriage When You Felt It Was All Settled*

For most people the decision to marry is as drastic and life-shaping as any decision they ever make. Even in our time, when many people back away casually and abruptly from marriage promises (promises that have often been casual and abrupt), few suppose that they do so safely. Even men and women who disbelieve in life-and-death promises are not surprised to find that marriage is something you do not walk away from intact. Or, to put it another way, anyone who *can* marry and then quit that union undamaged must be a person incapable of holding fast to others, and must have deeper problems to cope with than marital casualty.

For Christians who intend to pledge themselves to a lifelong partner, the choice is as close as most will come to negotiation with destiny.

How, then, can one be assured that one is choosing rightly? How can one trust the advice of others for a decision so personal and private? How can one be dispassionate about a matter so impassioned? How can one give one's heart away knowing, as even the lovestruck know, that the affairs of the heart are so chancy? There is a resolute sureness about the conviction that this is the person one wants to live with for the rest of one's life. But there are film stars who have had that resolute assurance eight times. Experience doesn't make this particular state of mind seem very reliable: divorce rates are even higher for second marriages than for first. For every couple proposing marriage, either their union will be an enduring one or they are lurching toward catastrophe. But no matter what it's worth, their proposal feels the same at the time they make it.

Is there no further assurance than their own feelings for couples who desire marriage and want to know if they are being sensible?

Not unnaturally the Christian tradition, which encourages men and women to bind themselves together for life, holds out to such couples a wisdom about how their inclination toward marriage can and should be put to the test.

Tradition in this matter is not very old, for it is only recently that women and men became free to marry someone they have personally known, fallen in love with, and chosen. And while this may seem to us the most natural and responsible prelude to a stable marriage, history tells us that our contemporaries' marriages are no more gracious and satisfying than those our ancestors undertook on their elders' say-so.

This leads us to the first helpful insight of the tradition: that one should doubt one's romance. I mean a principled and systematic doubt leading someone with the most unwavering and enthusiastic affection to distrust and examine those feelings: not because they are not strong enough but because, no matter how strong, they are not enough. It is a doubt of the head when the heart seems to have no doubts at all.

It is very difficult to put one's integrity to the test when one stands at the threshold of marriage and wants very much to enter. And those who speak for the tradition at this point know they sound like spoil-sports and kill-joys. But they also know that the man or woman who approaches engagement with real confidence that others can share is someone who was willing to pause just at the point of the most romantic momentum, to think about whether he or she could really deliver on the promises he or she was so eager to make—and whether the other person could do the same. When one's affections are really fierce, one must consider love as only making its debut: young, immature, unreliable. There is an irony here, that the lover who can help make the strongest marriage bond is the one who raises the hardest questions: is this the right person and the right time?

There is no guarantee of marital satisfaction, because it is a human endeavor that depends on continuing and growing dedication. But the decision to marry can be tested, if one is truly willing to risk a negative answer. The closest one can come to certainty is by assuming that one can't be certain, and by exposing oneself to the hard questions, the frank comments. In our culture, at least, men and women will continue to marry on the promptings of their hearts. But these can be trusted only by those who distrust them.

It is certainly unnerving for a person who considers himself all but engaged to find the fiancée-elect suddenly drawing back for a thoroughly new look at him. But it is the surest sign that she takes both him and their proposal of life together as seriously as she should. There is always something to be learned from how one's partner can tolerate a sober reconsideration.

## The Right Time, The Right Kind of Time

What issues ought be raised? A first is the need for time. One couple I know met when she was nursing him in a military hospital. Theirs was a wartime wedding, after only two months, but a good marriage, now nearly forty years old. Another couple of friends married only two weeks after they met, and they are still together, though not without stress. Although those may have been good marriages, I doubt that they were wise ones. Couples who marry on short notice usually do so because they do not want to take a good look. Most do not like what they see later when they cannot avoid looking. Those few who can keep their marriages together have to undergo a rediscovery and reacceptance of one another that is more demanding than many could endure.

For a couple to choose each other responsibly they must have spent adequate time together: adequate enough for them to know. For most folks this will mean years. There are indeed some people who can be known in months or even in weeks, but the reason for that is obvious (to everyone else). A sign in a motorcycle shop once caught my eye: "If you have a ten dollar head, buy a ten dollar helmet." Similarly, if all you have within you can be displayed in a few weeks or months, then by all means court that long and be assured that you will marry someone of equal depth. Some people are so light-weight that they could walk across flypaper and never stick. But any person who wants to know and be known through and through will want to wait and see.

The time is necessary, not to see whether the person is suited to you, but to determine whether both of you have the maturity and character to marry anyone.

It is important to have enough non-romantic time together. Whenever a couple is socially involved they are entertaining and being entertained . . . or pretending to do so. They are attending to one another, and so they are generally at their best. But the best is not what it is best to know. What one needs, in addition to time spent looking at one another, is time spent side by side, looking at other things. There are some things in another's personality that we can see only out of the corner of our eye. There are things two people can see and learn about one another when they are preparing and serving a dinner to guests that they could never see when they go out together for dinner. Painting a porch, filling out a tax return, tutoring children or working in an election campaign can offer people a peripheral vision of character in their co-workers that the direct gaze of dating may never reveal. We disclose ourselves best when we don't notice we are on view. That is why people need all kinds of time together.

Time spent apart can be revealing too. Fonder is not the only thing that absence makes the heart grow into. Some people, for instance, cling close in circumstances of loneliness and separation. Put them back where they are once again surrounded by friends and occupied by work, and their romance sometimes fades. Conversely, a woman might wonder why her beau could always warm and brighten to her whenever they are together, but now that he is two thousand miles away he cannot put pen to paper. The Marriage Encounter movement has induced thousands of couples to open themselves better to one another through writing than had been possible in conversation. And many separated courting couples have found that correspondence drew much more honesty out of them than Ma Bell ever did.

## What Are They Like at Home?

Another test that couples need is to see one another in their native habitats. A young man working in Manhattan may assume a character quite different from what he grew into back in Minnesota. And if a woman is content to make her first trek back to Minnesota to announce their engagement to his family, she may be getting there too late. The age at which most people marry is a time when some have pulled about as far away from the values of their upbringing as they will ever go. Shortly after that, when they begin to face the issues and responsibilities their parents faced before them, it is remarkable how the most out-of-harness people will home in on the very things that were held in high regard in their parents' home. I have known many young adults to rebel against strong-minded parents, and then have a marriage, a mortgage and a couple of children settle them right back into character: a character very much their own yet amazingly marked with the family crest.

If your fiancé takes you home to mother, and then you see him telling mother only half the story—or half of most stories—you should then be sure that he will lie to you too. And if your fiancée has no friend but you, or friends you do not much like, or if she is ready to leave aside her own friends and take on yours instead, what is it about her that seems to have you as its unique admirer? And if her mother neither has nor gives people peace unless she has her own way, take a good look at the daughter to make sure she is any different. And if your intended has no civil words for the brothers and sisters he spent all those years growing up with, how did he suddenly soften and become so charming to a stranger like yourself?

As long as one is bringing one's special friend home, one does well to ask one's family and friends what they would think of such a marriage. I would estimate that the average person has to be married for a good long time— say, three to five years—before the person's spouse could have a closer knowledge of him or her than the person's parents and siblings do. But how many men or women today have the desire or the nerve to present a prospective partner to their family or their most respected friends long enough for these closest people to offer their views on the union?

And how many parents or friends are willing to say what they think, even if asked? One daughter of a large and close family drifted off into her own world and soon became pregnant by a fellow student whom she then proposed to marry. Her parents and siblings showed her a solid front of affectionate support, but one by one they traveled across the country to tell her that, for what it was worth, they did not believe her fiancé was bound to her by anything very profound, nor that either one was yet mature enough to justify a marriage at that time. She was unable to meet their objections or even to think about them with much composure, and each time she simply responded by saying she knew it would be best to marry. They persisted, even up to the week of the wedding, in their attempts to talk her out of it. The wedding did take place; they put on a brave face and attended; and for years afterward they were cordial with her when she brought her child, and then her children, home for "weekends" and told them how miserable she was. When their younger sister announced her engagement to a young man they all liked, there was a wave of new, but different, dismay in the family. All her life this sister had in been the habit of throwing fierce tantrums with obscene shouting when she was thwarted at home. This was a side of her the young man had never seen, nor possibly suspected, but it would surely come to grace his home not long after their honeymoon. This time the family held its tongue. Or, more precisely, they shared their views among themselves. They all regretted what was about to befall their future son- and brother-in-law, but to him they said not a word. And since no one had the stomach for the sister's ill-tempered scenes, the family let her go her way. She had rejected an unflattering truth, and she was likely to continue to do that in her marriage.

Not every family is understanding, not every courter is headstrong. But many families who do have some perspective to share are never asked their views of an intended marriage, and feel they would be intruding to put them forward uninvited. So they all talk together quietly. Everyone is in the know except the one person who has most need to know, but does not have the nerve to ask.

Although I do not understand why, it seems that a family member or friend who is estranged can frequently offer the shrewdest comments on a prospective partner. So often they have the most galling knowledge of our failings. However well or awkwardly one gets along with them, though, one's family and gutsy friends will have sentiments and assessments about one's possible partner that one should be brave enough to hear.

## Be No Stranger to Your Partner's Mind

When a close friend comes by to talk over his or her ripening intention to marry, I like to ask what the partner's politics are. There is a deep craving to hold certain commitments in common between a husband and a wife. I do not think that politics need be one of those points of necessary unity. But if a man is on the brink of asking a woman to marry him and cannot tell me in what party she is registered nor how she stands on the major issues before the government, then I wonder how many other serious matters they may not have explored. Welfare programs, race relations, ecumenism, public education, taxation, military expenditures—none of this is what holds husbands and wives together. Nor will a disagreement—even a serious disagreement—in these matters necessarily destroy a marriage. Yet these are things they must have the character to explore, argue, negotiate. And if their companionship has not led them to a level where matters of this sort are frankly and enjoyably debated, one must wonder whether the companionship has any mind in it.

You cannot draw close enough to a person only by spending time with that person alone, and you cannot come to know a person by conversing only about each other. A courtship is insubstantial if the partners have not tested one another's reasoning on the substantial issues of the day. For one thing, one must discover whether one's friend can reason at all, or whether he or she is willing to hold and defend a position in the face of disagreement from someone very dear. If the reaction to debate is either a feisty, ego-entangled irritation or a readiness to abandon any position that would invite contention, then any prospective partner has a great deal to worry about. I have seen couples fall into a group animatedly debating something like anti-Semitism or foreign aid policy, and come away with astonishment over what they had seen for the first time in partners with whom they had thought themselves quite intimate.

A man and a woman do not assure themselves of a sound marriage just because they agree on most things. Nor does disagreement threaten their ability to live together in peace. What they do need is enough character, enough self-possession, to explore issues freely and inquiringly to the point where they *can* differ, and still enjoy a friendship that is loyal enough to survive these disagreements.

It is even more surprising to find people engaged without yet having sounded out one another's deepest convictions about matters they *will* later have to agree on. Religion, childbearing, careers, financial outlay and savings, place of residence, in-laws, vacations: these are matters about which a family has to be at peace. That does not mean they all have to be bargained for in an elaborate prenuptial contract. A young man and woman told me they would soon be marrying: he would study law and she would work to support them for three years; then she would take two years to secure her architect's license; they would have their first child in the middle of their sixth year; then they would move to a city ideal for his practice; in the eighth year she would resume her work, etc. etc. I had to ask myself what an untimely pregnancy or a broken hip or a miscarriage would do to that plan of life. They were entering an arrangement, not a marriage. I imagined the wedding commencing at 0900 hours EST . . . No journey which two people walk together, along with their children and their parents and their siblings and their children's spouses and their co-workers and their employers, can be calculated all that much in advance.

What courting couples can do, and should do, and what they so often seem to avoid doing, is to inquire seriously into each other's preferences or beliefs or commitments in advance. One particularly juvenile example may serve to illustrate. I recall one Ann Landers advice column which went something like this:

Dear Ann Landers:

I am 18 years old. My boyfriend and I have been going together now for three years, and naturally we have become intimate. I have been on the pill regularly, and this amounts to quite an expense [which it was then, in the middle 1960's]. Up till now I have been paying for it myself, but it seems to me that this is an expense my boyfriend should help with. I can't think of any way to ask him without sounding selfish. Please help.

Perplexed.

Dear Perplexed:

By all means keep on paying for the pills. You certainly don't want to have a child by someone you can't even discuss money with.

Ann Landers.

How possible is it to be intimate and never know one another's mind on the concrete matters of life together? How can so many marry and later ask for annulments on grounds that they were surprised to discover their spouses never wanted children? Marriages have exploded in anger when a husband bullied his wife into aborting their child or found she had done so without his knowledge and consent. In either case the outrage came as a total surprise to her. I know women destroyed by their husbands' abrupt refusal to allow them control over even household expenses, and men whose wives simply stepped over their children on their way to work.

None of these serious and agonizing differences had come to light beforehand. Why not? So often, because the couples sensed areas of conflict and avoided them, assuring themselves that they could be "worked out later." Later is the time when much will need to be worked out, and it will be too late.

This is not as much a private matter as it sounds, between two individuals. Time was when you could assume what a person's fundamental convictions were by the community he or she belonged to. Quakers were pacifists, Catholics married for life and Baptists didn't drink, just as Austrians skied and Irish drank. In our time it takes a more patient search to find what community of values a friend draws upon, or whether that person is sustained by no community at all. It is all the harder to know someone when it is so difficult to figure where he or she is coming from.

If a man and woman have not opened their minds to one another, long before they decide to marry, on these issues they will later have to agree on, then later on those issues may no longer be mutually resolvable. They will be settled by bullying. To avoid that, a sensible person will want to use his or her courtship to interrogate a partner on all manner of matters. If a couple cannot take that, they are no more intimate than the pair of eighteen-year-olds.

## You Get What You Deserve

It may seem that these tests are all intended to save people from choosing a poor marriage mate, and to protect good people from being victimized by bad ones. Not so. Good people don't usually make poor marriage choices, and sound people are not usually victimized by defective spouses. In fact, I am amazed at how consistently people get what they deserve in marriage. That is not to say that men and women instinctively pick mates with similar patterns of strengths and faults. Often they do not match at all. But people usually pick people with about the same measure of strength and fault as themselves.

This does not always show, for some faults are much more obvious than others which are equally serious. Some faults make more noise and kick more dirt in folks' eyes than other, quieter faults do. But at close quarters, over time, there are tiny faults that can drive people to despair. For instance, we are all quickly alerted to a bossy person, the kind who is always moving onto others' turf, and who will tell you quickly what someone else wants without giving the other person the first say about it: the kind of fellow who is ready to tell everyone else how to do his or her job. Fewer of us are apt to notice that the partner of this take-over sort of person is usually one who avoids decisions, doesn't like to say what she thinks best, and never objects to what the other wants to do . . . until the next day when she may play the martyr with sympathetic friends. No one has a right to complain of what they permit. Parents lament their teenagers' drinking and do nothing to stop it. Administrators deplore the unprofessional behavior of their employees and do nothing to discipline them. And, in couples facing marriage or living in it, for every person who exploits there is another who invites exploitation. We are much quicker to spot and blame the former. It is my belief that they are mates and equals for each other.

Givers and takers have an almost charmed capacity for mating. Takers are people who always get their own way. Some of them were indulged throughout their youth and somehow began to believe that this world exists for them. When they hunger, they expect to be fed, and if no one leaps to feed them they are not only famished; they are frustrated, angry. Others, apparently the victims of deprived childhoods, now consider it only fair to compensate by elbowing their way more energetically up to the trough of life with gusto, by easing everyone else aside. Whatever their upbringing, all takers have a selfish sense of justice that drives away other people—except givers, who gravitate toward them. Givers are people who sacrifice everything to serve someone: what they sacrifice is not only their own convenience, but their own judgment, their dignity and honor, and their own sense of what is life-giving, too. This phony generosity serves people's desires, not their needs. Almost every time, we see the taker as the bully, and think of the giver as the victim. But I have come to think that they are equally destructive, and a dangerous combination, like sadism and masochism.

Occasionally we all meet a family in which one partner clearly takes advantage of the other: the beaten wife, for instance, is abused by an alcoholic husband. We sympathize with the one and deplore the other. But we ought to ask what weaknesses led her, years before, to overlook the first signs of his undependable character. Usually we shall find that they each had a hand in ruining the other.

A women in her later thirties took up with a lawyer who had decided that he wanted to become a writer. Together they found a house in the country and moved in. He wrote and she provided for their home, doing all she could to make his work easier. When the year was drawing to its end they took a journey of several weeks together, and it was then that their conversation turned toward marriage. By the time they had returned it was a definite decision. He needed to explain things first to his family, so he went home to make arrangements. She telephoned her closest friends to tell them joyfully that after so many years and disappointments she had finally found a man who was kind and considerate, and with whom she had a profound relationship. No call came the first day, nor the second, and on the third day she telephoned his home. A sister explained that he couldn't come to the phone, and did not want her to call; he would be contacting her. After a good long think she got in her car and drove cross-country to his family home. Again the sister met her at the door and explained he would not see her. But she insisted on waiting in the front room. Finally he came down and told her they would not be marrying, and that he wanted her off the property, pronto. She left, and went into a horrible depression.

Finally she got help, and with her counselor came to see how a pattern had been repeating itself in her life. Once

she had become attached to a Japanese man, and had therefore studied the Japanese language for two full years.
Another man had been into animal breeding, so she took
courses in genetics. A third had had fascinating rural Mis-
sissippi roots, and that had led her into the lore of the back
country of the state. In every case she had thrown herself
into the interests of her male companion, and in every case
she had been tossed out at the end. Then she recalled that
during this last affair, and indeed during the others too, virtually all visitors had been at her invitation: in fact, none
of her partners had had a circle of friends.

After each rejection she would go into fits of self-
hatred: she was worthless, unattractive, a vile person.
Sometimes this would pass over into an angry, male-hating
phase: men were mean, cruel, exploitative. But now it was
dawning on her that she had been throwing herself self-
abasingly at any man who would allow her to become a
slave, and with uncanny aim she threw herself at men who
expected just this kind of abasement. She began to realize
that men who could spend a half-hour of initial conversation without asking a single question about herself, except
perhaps for their own purposes ("Is your car here?"
"Would you have enough money for us to catch dinner
tonight?")—these were men she could do without. She
began to see how egocentric her own attitude had been. By
putting herself at any man's total beck and call she had
been avoiding the challenge to be adult. Only by meeting
them on equal terms could she begin to learn to love. The
people who pack all those free lunches are just as caught up
in themselves as the people who consume them.

The problem is not for strong people to avoid weak
partners, because strong people are not usually attracted to

weak people. It is weak people who usually seek partners with complementary weaknesses. If they put themselves to the test boldly and truthfully enough, they will find that what they have to avoid is neither this particular candidate nor any other particular one. They have to avoid all candidates for marriage until they can find the strength to give and receive love steadfastly. Givers and takers and other people of matched weaknesses are both victims and victimizers. So, in examining a prospective marital mate one is often looking in the mirror for a reverse image of one's own readiness for matrimony. One had better take a good look.

## Pre-Marital Sex

There is another test the tradition holds out to us. To face life together a couple must have experienced forgiveness and reconciliation. They must have given and taken enough offense to see how each copes with serious anger and humiliation and stubbornness. This has a purpose beyond showing a couple how firm their friendship is on the rebound, or how much at risk it is from disagreement, misunderstanding or offense. It provides them with a school of reconciliation, a task each will need to become good at, no matter whom they choose to marry.

I think of some couples whose most valuable experience during courtship was a vigorous quarrel or an offense. Sometimes it led them to a parting of the ways, offering a foretaste of the bitterness that married couples suffer when they are estranged. Sometimes apologies are slow in coming, for the more we count on someone the angrier we are when he or she lets us down. Couples who have not had to

forgive one another some painful failures do not seem sobered enough to be married well.

There is one activity of marriage, however, that Christian wisdom has warned against as a prelude to marriage:
sex. I have already tried to portray the traditional conviction that sex ought to mean what marriage ought to mean:
that a man and woman have given their lives to one
another, for better or for worse, until death; that neither
now has any privacy from which the other is excluded; that
each accepts the other's children. My purpose in returning
to the subject is not simply to re-emphasize that sex outside
marriage is wrong, but to urge that sex before marriage is
especially detrimental.

Others have observed that most pre-marital sex is not
"pre" anything, at least not "pre-"marriage. It is a euphe-
mism for extra-marital sex. I dissent from the common
view that sex is all right as long as it is in anticipation of
matrimony, or that it is less deplorable for an engaged couple to be sleeping together than for people to be sleeping
around promiscuously. On the contrary, the tradition
argues that sex is perhaps most dangerous and costly when
it does lead to marriage, a good deal more so than a one-
night stand, which is not nearly so liable to illusions.

When a man and woman do not belong to one another
but are joined in a union as powerful as sex, they become
two in one flesh without being two in one life. If they are
involved in a continuing relationship, it is almost impossible for them not to become convinced that they belong to
one another. You can hardly go through the motions of
belonging to another over a period of time without that
experience summoning up the feeling that the two of you

are at one. For two persons approaching marriage seriously this illusion is disastrous. At the very time when they most need the freedom it takes to give up one's entire life, they are undermining that freedom by artificially arousing the illusion that they already belong to each other. It is not the sex itself which is so destructive. But, like alcoholism, it can aggravate every existing problem.

On their wedding day a man and woman give their lives, their intimacy, their goods to one another. They "begin [their] married life with the voluntary and complete surrender of [their] individual lives in the interest of that deeper and wider life which [they] are to have in common . . . one in mind, one in heart, one in affections." This is an agreement after which one is never again on one's own. But the agreeing itself is an individual venture. Indeed, when the man and the woman, each in the first person singular, give themselves over to each other, it is their last great singular act.

It is also an awesome act, an act not everyone is capable of. There are many human beings who cannot give themselves away because they do not possess themselves in the first place. They roam impulsively instead of pursuing a course they have determined. And if they find themselves at the altar, they enact their wedding without that inner freedom it would require really to part with their selves. The trouble with pre-marital sex is its power to impair this freedom of choice. At the very time a couple need the clearest view of one another and must be free enough from each other to decide whether to embrace each other for life, they are held in an embrace which makes them feel as though they have already done so, and so their energy to face the life decision is weakened.

Courtship is a time when the characters of two people should be open to mutual exploration. This is the most important time when natural antagonisms, poor temper, boredom and superficiality need to be felt. When their relationship has become sexual there is a strong temptation to turn to sexual affection just when the personal companionship becomes difficult or boring. Sex then interrupts the ordinary dynamic of the man and woman's growing friendship . . . and anaesthetizes the need to grow further.

It is ironic and painful to observe how often a couple will begin to decide on marriage a few weeks after they have begun to have sex together, and how often a close observer can foresee that their forward motion into friendship, challenge and maturity is stalled at almost the same time. Of all the dislocations that can affect courtship, sex wreaks great havoc precisely because while giving the illusion of union it forestalls the hard business of two independent persons, knowing they continue to be independent, learning to draw close.

To couples preparing for marriage and wanting an account of our tradition's stored wisdom on this, I try to explain why Christians have persistently believed sex was both untrue and deceptive for men and women determined to marry. On occasion a man and woman will tell me that they had been sexually involved but that, after reflecton, they have discontinued their sexual activity. I am always amazed at this, for it is so painful for a couple whose intimacy has become sexual to fast from that communion. But invariably they have told me their friendship was reinvigorated. No longer able to substitute sex for personal exchange, they found themselves once more creative in entertaining one another, and more frank and truthful in confronting their shortcomings. Without exception, they told me their courtship became even closer without the sexual involvement.

## Moving In Is Not Moving On

Special difficulties arise when a couple move in together. The popular theory is that they are wise to try out marriage before taking any irrevocable decisions. What better test of marriage? The theory founders on the simple fact that the one thing distinctive about marriage, the one thing that sets it apart from all other romantic relationships, the one thing that makes it so hazardous, is precisely what living together cannot anticipate: an irrevocable decision. A cohabitating couple is, if anything, left to guess what marriage might be like, for commitment is what makes marriage, and commitment is what they have purposely avoided.

The practice, apart from the theory, has problems of its own. Today when a couple decide to move in together they are clearly deciding not to marry. They purposefully hesitate to commit themselves. They enter a relationship that is deliberately non-binding. They dwell together, say, for five years. Then, those who have not left one another often decide to have a wedding. It may be brought on by pregnancy, or by a desire to relieve the discomfort of their families, or to give some acceptable public status to their union. But after years of being together it is awkward for them to say that they are going to get married. That would repudiate what they had built together, or at least it would cast their experience into a tentative light. When they are given a free hand in the design of the wedding ritual they

tend to make it clear that they are not there to make any
new bond between each other: they are only giving public
notice and celebration of a private bond that somehow
already exists.

The question arises: what does exist between a man
and woman who, for whatever reasons, explicitly decided
against marriage? And their problem is that they end up
"officially" married without there having been an explicit
and unambiguous commitment openly made. They have
sidestepped into marriage. Their wedding is intended to
reaffirm something, but that thing is what they have purposely avoided affirming beforehand. Every cohabiting
couple I have known has had to face this handicap. While
they lived together unmarried they could not accept a commitment. But when they then wanted to marry they could
not quite accept the fact that no steadfast commitment yet
existed. Only those who are truly free can commit themselves, and this freedom is a wrench to the sensibilities of
men and women who have been going through the motions
of belonging while never quite handing their selves over.

## No One Can Have To Get Married

If there is one prelude to marriage which is even less
auspicious and more menacing than cohabitation it is pregnancy. The state of mind of almost every party to a mar-
riage-cum-pregnancy is deranged. My own observation is
that there is nothing—absolutely nothing—which pregnancy damages that marriage can repair. As a priest I particularly resent the undiscriminating readiness of some colleagues to preside at such marriages. At a shotgun marriage

the shotgun should be fired at the clergyman, who ought to have known better when no one else did.

Everything is in turmoil. Parents are anxious to rescue their social reputations, and somehow imagine that their neighbors and friends either do not have calendars or cannot count. Or, for fear of alienating their children, they agree to anything their children say they want. Or, deploring their intention to marry, they either turn upon them in rage or fall into mournful silence and never once tell their children what they see in store for them. The pregnant woman is often beside herself (unless the pregnancy was intended to force matrimony), and anxious before all else to be sheltered. She can be told that the enormous majority of such marriages break up—and often after only a few years—and that she is most likely to end up with a child that has a father's name but no father to go with it. She will listen to it all and she will hear none of it, and convince herself that a wedding will solve everything. Ask her to consider the child's welfare, to give the child to a childless family that is established and ready and anxious for a child, rather than consigning the child to be raised by an eventually single parent, and you might as well holler into the wind, for she will most often choose to keep the child, much like a Raggedy Ann. She will speak of the child's interests but she will feel her own. The father usually gets little sympathy, and he knows it. He can't get pregnant. Everyone knows he can walk away from both woman and child, and the unspoken accusation creates a pathological guilt that often leads him into marriage just to purge himself of suspicion and to demonstrate his sense of responsibility.

Responsibility is exactly what is absent from the whole proceeding. The couple has the most explicit recollection that they had already decided on marriage before this all happened, a recollection as reliable as that of a Jersey City politician before a grand jury. In more than several decades of pastoral experience I have not known half a dozen pregnant couples who retained sufficient sanity to enact the serious, free, reflective decision we call Christian marriage. It is especially sad when family and friends know that marriage at that point would be irrational, but want to be loving and supportive. The couple then misread all this affection as approval, and hustle them all into a bizarre ceremony that everyone marches through in formal attire, then goes home to weep.

What Christian marriage requires is what those unfortunate men and women so often lack: a self-possession firm enough for them to give themselves away freely.

This is really the issue for any person drawn to marry. What is more demanding than marriage, in which one lays down his or her life for a friend? And what is more turbulent than the experiences surrounding the decision to marry? This pledge, according to Christian tradition, is too burdensome to be fulfilled alone. We all need a community and a family to support us, and to hold us to it, and to shoulder the load when we falter.

This is also true of the decision itself. It is too perilous, and too many others have a stake in it, for this community to abandon us to our own private designs and desires. If we call them to celebrate with us on the day of our marriage we should call on them to deliberate with us beforehand. A lifetime decision we are afraid to expose to be tested on the wisdom of others is too furtive a decision to be trusted.

# 3 *Bonds of Promise, Bonds of Blood*

Curiosity drew me on a five-year journey during which I studied abortion and infanticide. After decades as an invited guest in other people's consciences I had considered myself beyond surprise. This, however, was to be a research project that would surprise me with surprises. I was a teacher who learned a great deal. And what I learned was mostly about parents and children.

I discovered that deep within the movement for abortion freedom lies the conviction that no unwanted child should ever be born. I agreed. Every child, I believed, has a claim on our love: not only our own children, but those whose families cannot or will not receive them. Yet here were people who believed that if a mother would not welcome her child, the child would be better off if eliminated before birth. Here I very much disagreed. The same distance separates supporters of apartheid from partisans of racial equality, who both proclaim that no unwanted blacks should exist in South Africa, but have devastatingly different dreams of how that might be achieved.

The public wisdom in America, I learned from *Time* magazine, was that "without legal and affordable abortion, many lives in progress are hopelessly ruined; the unwanted children very often grow up unloved, battered, conscienceless, trapped and criminal." Americans United for Separation of Church and State said: "It is a low form of cruelty to insist ruthlessly on bringing into the world a child for whom there is no welcome. . . . " The same message came from the president of The Minnesota Abortion Rights Council: "Among the 800,000 unplanned, unwanted children born every year in the U.S., many become loved and wanted. Unfortunately, many others end up as battered children, delinquents and criminals. Studies of battered children reveal a high percentage of unmarried and unwanted pregnancy, or forced marriage among the abusive parents." It was not this person's implication that in order to be wanted a child must have been planned, nor even her saying that 800,000 unwanted children are born here each year, a statistic which she contrived for the occasion, that snagged my attention. It was her argument that exterminating the unloved was a good way to clear up the hostility toward children in our land.

## Wanted Children May Not Be Welcome Children

Still, all this dogmatic assurance that unwanted children were mistreated led me to the experts on child abuse. Here a surprise awaited me. Dr. E. F. Lenoski of the University of Southern California Medical School had found that battered or abused children were much more likely even than normal children to have been born from desired pregnancies. They were more likely to be of legitimate birth, and to have mothers who displayed satisfaction with their pregnancies. Here was a suggestion that abused children were, in some grotesque way, *wanted* children.

Ray Helfer, one of the leading authorities in the field, has explained that abusive parents are themselves often the victims of estrangement and abuse as children, and they crave a child as one person whom they can cherish and from whom they can find satisfaction. "Many young mothers who had every desire to get pregnant, with great expectations that the baby would resolve one of their many problems, find themselves even worse off than before. Their baby does not—or is not able to—meet these needs." Helfer's colleague, C. Henry Kempe, who coined the term "the battered child syndrome," observes: "Basic in the abuser's attitude toward infants is the conviction, largely unconscious, that children exist in order to satisfy parental needs."

Quite contrary to the popular claim, parents likely to abuse their children are *unlikely* to consider abortion. Aborting parents may not desire their children, but abusing parents do desire them, though in a pathetic way. If the two groups of parents have anything in common, according to another child abuse expert, Brandt Steel, it is "the assumption that the rights, desires, and ideas of the adult take full precedence over those of the child, and that children are essentially the property of parents who have the right to deal with their offspring as they see fit, without interference."

Abortion and abuse stood together, I found, not opposed. Both stemmed from a conviction that children are the possessions of their parents, to be disposed of in conformity with their parents' interests. Here was a new and provocative insight.

Next I was caught up short by a view that even if infanticide is wrong, it is not very wrong, because its victim is so insignificant. I had been raised to think that crimes were

more detestable when their victims were weak or unde-
fended. It was particularly heartless to mug an elderly
woman, or to defraud a refugee, or to abuse a lower-level
employee. As Gandhi wrote, "I hold that the more helpless
a creature, the more entitled it is to protection by man from
the cruelty of man."

But to my astonishment here were distinguished schol-
ars arguing that killing infants is only mildly objectionable
because infants are not yet our equals. To do away with the
unborn is still less troubling, since they lag still farther
behind our grown status. The same for the hopelessly senile
or others who have no claim to "the respect due to normal
human beings." Glanville Williams, a Cambridge law pro-
fessor who was very influential in the abortion movement
in both his country and ours, agrees with this perspective:
"Infanticide appears to our generation to be a crime less
heinous than ordinary murder.... 'The victim's mind is
not sufficiently developed to enable it to suffer from the
contemplation of approaching suffering or death.... It
leaves no gap in any family circle, deprives no children of
their breadwinner or their mother, no human being of a
friend, helper or companion.'" I was puzzled by this doctrine that it was worse to take on someone your own size
than to pick on a kid.

There were other bewilderments to follow. I had
known that youngsters born with various handicaps often
perished before leaving hospital nurseries, because of decisions agreed upon by their parents and their doctors. Others were abandoned by their families to institutions. I imagined impoverished couples undone by the expense of
keeping a handicapped child at home. The evidence suggests, however, that it is the affluent, more than the poor,

who may be willing to free themselves of their handicapped young. As one doctor reports: "Couples who are success-oriented and have high expectations for their children are likely to institutionalize their mentally deficient offspring rather than keep them at home. The argument that mongoloids raised in the home perform better than those raised in an institution is rarely persuasive with such parents." I thought this was peculiar: men and women with the means to provide their needy children with all that money can buy were withholding the things that are beyond price.

When medical staffs volunteer to eliminate unwanted infants by denying them either nourishment or medical treatment, it can be quite painful—for them, the staff. Dr. Anthony Shaw, who has reported that the liquidation of handicapped infants is common practice, complains of this strain. "Standing by and watching a salvageable baby die is the most emotionally exhausting experience I know . . . a terrible ordeal for me and for the hospital staff—much more than for the parents who never set foot in the nursery."

It was difficult to understand why the doctors accepted this task of destruction, which they described as "arduous, agonizing, distasteful." Since no further medical care was to be allowed, why not present the parents with their infant and send them home to starve him or her themselves?

The next surprise which lay in wait cast some light back upon this one. Rosalyn Darling has studied the problems of parents of children with such chronic handicaps as congenital blindness, spina bifida, etc. Most parents, she found, were coping. They would have wished their children free of these disabilities, but they cherished the youngsters and would not wish to have been deprived of them. Their dissatisfaction was not with their children but with their physicians. Many had changed doctors in search of one who would take an interest in their youngsters.

The doctors admitted that they felt unprepared to treat patients with chronic defects. "A world-view that primarily involves sick people who get better may not leave room for the chronically ill or incurable patient whose defect cannot be 'fixed,'" wrote Darling. "'Success,' in this view, seems somehow to be equated with complete normalcy of function, and the chronically ill or disabled present a moral dilemma to the physician so oriented. As my findings have indicated, a life defined by physicians as intolerable might come to be defined in a very different way by parents."

Even personnel skilled in physical rehabilitation or education of the retarded confess a falling off of interest when their efforts no longer yield measurable improvement. What is one to think of helping professionals who would not care simply to care?

It is disheartening to witness these and other similar attitudes toward children: children unborn, blighted, helpless, unwanted. Was it sentimentality that made me so affronted by these attitudes? Or naïveté? Or simple ignorance? It is difficult to know. In any case, these points of surprise came in time to form a pattern that gradually made larger sense.

The picture was sobering. History, as we can recover it, discloses a frequent disposition to abuse and annihilate children when they are not welcomed. This is not done only by psychotically hysterical mothers or by underworld quacks. It is accomplished by your neighbors down the street and by medical school professors who describe the process in learned journals.

Ours is a country in which it can be very risky to be very young, and where only the narrowest of margins assures children of love and protection. The medical profession struggles to reduce the rate of infant mortality, but this kind of infant mortality is itself the work of physicians.

This raises heavy questions for every man and woman among us, including those who will never raise a hand to smite or slay a child. And the more so for those who believe their Parent disclosed his presence to them by sending a Child, and who believe in a Lord who said we could draw close only if we came to him as children

## Parenting by Choice

What might a Christian think, in a world where children have such little value for so many of our fellow adults?

A three-year-old girl, supplied with a sack of sandwiches and toys, is found on the steps of a Sunday school, abandoned by her twenty-two-year-old mother and her mate. A newborn infant, with umbilical cord still attached, is heard crying at the bottom of a trash chute, discarded by her teenage mother. About one and a half million offspring are aborted annually by American mothers. One out of every seven deaths in the nursery for newborn children at one prominent university medical center results from purposeful extermination, and the doctors who disclose the fact become media personalities.

However terrifying we might consider this readiness to reject and victimize one's own young, it is too common an act and attitude for us to think of it as something abnormal, or freakish. On the contrary, it is all around us. We should be under no illusions that parental instinct alone will provide welcome and safety for children.

Several years ago a friend took me out to a stable to inspect her mare's new foal. Mare and colt were let out to pasture, and I marveled at the mother's persistence in not letting him more than a few feet from her. I had not thought her to be a very friendly animal, but here she was, seized by a fierce maternal possessiveness that extinguished every other instinct. After five months of this, the mare had her foal taken from her to be weaned, in an awful scene. But two weeks later neither mother nor colt seemed to recognize one another. It had all been a melodrama of hormones.

With the possible exception of the daytime soaps, human beings are not governed by such animal instincts. Prolactin and other hormones may draw a mother to nurture her newborn, but instinct alone isn't enough for the lifelong duties of parenthood. Nurture is natural only in virtuous human beings, and children require many virtues in their parents that are diverse and disciplined. Indeed, to be a decent parent demands a more-than-decent maturity that is generous and sound.

The acceptance of children is a willful act. It is a choice. It can be a duty. When one is with child, one is obliged to provide for that child. Nevertheless, not every necessity is necessarily taken care of. And this is one obligation which women and men will meet only by self-determination. There are adults in great number who do not rise to the occasion. It is no small thing to receive a small person into one's life.

Christians have reflected upon family in ways that should make this clear to them. We have observed that the instinct for mating runs up against other vigorous instincts like random sexual hunger, or against character problems like greed, ambition, and laziness. It is one thing for a person to bring another to bed, and quite another to let another surely and safely into one's life. This is a matter of commitment more than of chemistry: in fact, the commitment will sometimes break down the chemistry.

It is an old Christian notion that to accept someone else as yours, for better or for worse, until death, requires a motivation and stamina and patience that only God could give. Men and women can mate or marry without these gifts but they may not stay together long. If this is how we view bonds of promise between spouse and spouse, no less can be true of the bonds of blood between parent and child. On a Christian view of things, only the Father can enable us to be gracious enough to do something as natural as being good fathers or mothers. And if we can do that, is there any humanly greater thing which we cannot do?

We should not be surprised that so many women and men care more for their own pleasure than for their own children. A devoted parent is an occasion for celebration, not just what you have a right to expect.

If Christians have a high though heavy sense of what parenting requires, it behooves us at least to invite others to share it. What might be the lineaments of such a vision?

## How Do We Need Children?

Christians believe that the sting of death has been relieved by a Messiah who was pierced for us. Jesus died at our hands to show us his love, a love he had from his Father and ours: a love stubborn enough to enfold children who turned their backs on him, and then turned upon him to destroy. The staying power of such a love, we believe, is not to be undone by death. We shall be close by him despite our deaths and because of his.

This hope frees us from children while at the same time it brings them more closely into our embrace. If all we can look forward to were destroyed by death, then we could have immortality in only two things: our accomplishments and our children. If we depend on children to give our lives remembrance after we are gone, then we shall be grooming and cultivating them with an eye to our own continuity and celebrity. But once we are freed from the need to ready our children as our own memorials, we can begin to serve them as persons in their own right.

Nowadays most of what we hear about relationships between and among people has to do with rights. This is true of the family too: we read about parents' rights, and children's rights. In the Christian tradition rights are not the most important aspect of parent-child relationships. Rights are important, of course, but we don't even start to think of them until our affairs are already quite disturbed. Rights are a fall-back consideration.

Needs bind us together before rights do. Much more are we bound together by needs. By this I mean less that children need parental care if they are to survive than that adults need children to care for if they are to survive. The Church has little lesson for us about how we can mature in adulthood if we have no young to be responsible for. Even vowed communities of Christian men and women celibates find the service of the junior members by their elders to be an essential need.

Like all needs, our need for children can become unhealthy. For instance, it is all too easy to consider children as a possession rather than as a trust. One can see a caricature of this in the Little League father who is unhappily working out his own ego needs through the performance of his young son ("How could you be stupid enough to drop that fly ball?"). His female counterpart is the majorette mother who drills her pre-adolescent daughter for tournaments like a Pomeranian for a dog show. When these children grow older and try to become independent, it might become apparent that the fathers' and mothers' attentions were more self-satisfying than gracious.

Real parental care, as we Christians try to understand and cultivate it, reaches beyond the needs and interests of our own children. This may give us second thoughts about the newer and expensive techniques now being developed to allow sterile couples to conceive. Behind the view that a couple's life is terribly damaged if they cannot physically produce "their own" offspring, there may be a feeling that children are a possession instead of a trust. Is it only coincidence that at the same time so many children are being deprived of either a family or of life itself rather than being given in adoption—as if a child would suffer if raised by any but its biological parent?

Our tradition of adoption rests on our belief that we must all share in parenting. None of us may rest if there are children in need of parents. And none of us may destroy children rather than sharing them with others who need and wish to take them in. Children are a treasure to be shared, not property to be withheld.

## Two Parents Are Not Enough

We are all meant to be godparents to the children of the world. Every youngster requires attention from dozens, even hundreds, of generous adults, and kindnesses and services beyond what his or her parents could ever provide. So are we all under obligation to exert ourselves for the care of one another's children. We are stewards of them all.

Justice for children requires a conscientious balance. One cannot slap one's own children into day-care to be free to get out and about, to a socially productive career. No one's children should have to pay the full price for their parents to be of help to others. But neither can one channel all one's ambitions into the development of one's own off-spring ("My son, the brain surgeon!"), for any child will crumple under that burden. Somehow we must care for our own without turning our backs on others'. We are no more than stewards of our own children, and no less than stewards of others'.

This Christian vision of childbearing is enough to make one blink. We need to have children to care for, in order to grow ourselves. We need to keep children, not as a possession but as a trust, not as an eventual credit to ourselves but as a credit to themselves. And in order to serve our own children selflessly we need to make other people's children an additional obligation on our care. This is no small calling.

I think that if we follow that Christ-call, we would inevitably display a favoritism for the handicapped. Jean Vanier founded L'Arche, a movement to encourage Christian families to form communities that take retarded persons in to live among them. He believes that the mentally handicapped thrive more in such a setting than in an institutional one. And he makes the even more startling claim that *we* thrive remarkably more if we have someone retarded living beside us, in our charge and care.

There are various crises in life that bring us stumbling into someone else's doorway. I have known young women, pregnant and partnerless, who have been welcomed into strangers' homes only to find that this proved the dearest year of their lives. Estrangement brought them a new and lifelong family. And I have known families that foster or adopt, and particularly families who take in youngsters who, because of race or handicap or age, go begging for a home. Those are the children who bring the biggest blessing with them, who bring more to parents and brothers and sisters because they bring more out of them.

I think that if we were to follow that Christ call, we would know it is our duty to be an example to others, to light a lamp for others to see children better, and to see themselves in a new light. I was instructed in the power of example by Dr. Germaine Greer whose book *The Female Eunuch* had discussed the ways we can diminish and degrade women. She became a leader in the feminist movement. But a decade later, when she journeyed to the East as a guest of the Family Planning Association of India, she was staggered by the experience, in exactly the opposite way from what had been expected.

In all the villages she visited, she said, she never found an unwanted child. Parents cherished their children because they had fought so hard against disease and malnutrition to have them. They looked upon Dr. Greer as an unfortunate woman because she had none. She couldn't explain her failure to have children except to say to that "in my society, there is no idea of continuum. In my society, the individual life is self-contained." And she added: "That village hardly knew the use of the word 'I'. It's 'we' every inch of the way."

Women who bear children gain seniority in their villages, she reported. "And they really have seniority. They were more important and more powerful in family affairs than the men were. The men were allowed the abstract discourse. The men were allowed sports. The women had the day-to-day running of the family. Nothing could be done without them."

When the family existed in America, she said, women's lives were more bearable. "But the American family was destroyed generations ago," she stated categorically, and that has taken away much of women's power.

Americans who advocate birth control for people in other cultures, she said, don't realize that not everyone has the American attitude toward sex. "In our society, sex is an indoor sport. We imagine that sexuality is the primary thing. But that's not the way it is in the rest of the world. The primary relationship is the family."

Dr. Greer said she doubts if we rightly understand the problem of overpopulation in the world. She returned to the example of the Indian village to make her point. "The entire village had squeezed into one half of a room, and had left the other half to me," she said. "When I looked at these people, I knew perfectly well who there were too many of. There were too many of me."

## Christians Have Different Ideas on Family

If the treasuring of family and of children in Hindu villages in India could give such profound pause to this woman of such strong convictions, we must ask whether Christian communities in America display the convictions we are supposed to possess about children and family, or whether we are simply blending into the landscape. If we lived up to our beliefs—openly and consciously—we would stand out like Lubavitcher Jews in Brooklyn, or Amish farmers in rural Pennsylvania, or Hare Krishna youngsters in the airports, or Jehovah's Witnesses ringing the doorbell.

If we lived out our deepest convictions about family we would startle both ourselves and our neighbors: repelling some, to be sure, but benefiting many. It is ironic that when we do take a stand on a family issue—abortion, for example—we arouse indignation because we are taken to be imposing and arrogant. All things considered, are we not really more timid than our convictions deserve?

To take the abortion conflict as an example: any convictions we have that are religious *ought* to show forth.
Instead of being bothered by the red-white-and-blue accusation that our faith is showing, we should be relieved that
it *is,* and confess to sadness if it were not. What could be
more embarrassing to Christians than to have it known that
on a crucial matter regarding the bearing of children, our
religious beliefs made us look like everybody else?

It is interesting that the same religious groups which
oppose abortion are the ones that place the highest value
on marriage. The ones who insist that unborn people be
protected, even at sharp sacrifice, are the ones who insist
that marriages be protected, even at sharp sacrifice. Those
who defend the union of man and woman are also defend-
ers of the bond between parents and children. It is the same
matter of fidelity: to live, to survive, we must stand by
those who belong to us by bonds of blood, just as we must
keep faith with those who belong to us by bonds of promise.

It is not so much a question of when a person's life
begins as it is a question of how we treat a person. Chris-
tianity says less about the value of human life than it does
about the value of human beings to our life. It says that we
have nothing better to do with our lives than to share them
with others. It says that when one person kills another, the
killer is killed, too—and in a more drastic way.

Christians hate killing because we know that we need
to sustain others' lives in order to live ourselves. It's not so
much that the unborn is human, but that he or she is our
brother or sister, and if we don't take care of our brothers
and sisters, we will die. The doctrine is more about me than
about him or her.

Christians don't have very peculiar teachings about whether the unborn are human, but we do know in a distinctive way that we are a community which needs to welcome children into the world.

How true, on this view of the matter, that no unwanted child should ever be born. And how true, on that view of the matter, that we, and not the child, must bear the cost and the burden of this conviction. And, how extravagantly Christian is that view of the matter.

## Bonds of Promise, Bonds of Blood

Bonds are more precious than relationships. In our tradition we have certain hopes that appear to some people as unrealistic. One of those hopes is that it is possible to make pledges and promises to one another that will bind us as closely as if we shared the same flesh and blood. That belief is not widely shared in our world. So I think the most distinctive belief in our family tradition is that bonds of promise can be as strong as bonds of blood. And it is our belief that teaches us, in turn, that bonds of blood are not to be selfish ties of tribal instinct, but biological links we ratify and transfigure by choice and love. They are a bondage that is liberating.

A second part of our "unrealistic" tradition is that people make these promises for better or for worse until death. When I use those words, you naturally think of the promises husbands and wives make to one another. But isn't that also a description of the promises children and their parents also make to one another?

What we will cherish most in the evening of our lives is not the relationships we have had, but the bonds we have made. We believe that family is not only a matter of relationships, but also one of bonds.

We have relationships with business associates, and what goes on between business associates is often very important. But these are not bonds. A number of people live together in what they call "meaningful relationships." These are not bonds. People leave college with friendships which will last a lifetime. These are truly meaningful relationships. They are not bonds.

A bond is where you have a handicapped child and you don't ask yourself how you're going to cherish the child. You already cherish the child.

A bond is where some people in your family are growing too old to take care of themselves. And you know they are yours. And you will take care of them.

When a phone rings and someone tells you there was a wreck, and your child is hurt, you don't think, "Shall I go?" You say, "I'm coming." You don't think. You go. That is a bond.

# 4 *Almost Too Much to Bear: On Children, and How They Raise Their Parents*

When we say "parents and children" we tend to picture a couple in their twenties or thirties, with the customary two or three children, probably at elementary school age or younger. But parenthood is a lifelong identity, and the parent-child relationship continues on throughout the lives of both parent and child. This same young couple will still be parents—and actively parents—when they are in their eighties and their children are grandparents. Parenthood does not lapse when one's children move onto their own. It really comes into its own only when one's children are adults.

And the parent-child relation need not always be colored by authority. One of the frustrations of being mother and father is that so much of the early experience of families demands firm parental control. When the time comes for tearing loose, for taking wing, for the children to gather their own privacy and autonomy about themselves—in short, when the end of command and control arrives—many fathers and mothers feel their parenthood taken away from them. They are at a loss to negotiate new ways of dealing with sons and daughters.

But parenthood should have more gifts to share than that: much of what parents offer is only available anyway in those years when their children are no longer dependent upon them. It is a mutual devastation if at the very age when the parent has the richest wisdom and perspective to share with his or her child, both have shut each other off in the belief that the family's unity is at an end now that they have quit the same roof.

A parent, no matter how mature, no matter what his or her degree of control, authority, or involvement, must be concerned for every feature of his or her child's life.

The parent-child bond is a lifelong one. It certainly outlives the immaturity of the children, and perhaps it even outlasts death. In the New Testament one of the Gospels says that after Jesus had died and risen and appeared for a time and then no longer appeared, his disciples began to reminisce about things that he had said during the days when they had walked together: things that then had gone over their heads. As his words came back to them they were able to think about them, to understand them as they did not and could not understand them before. They were challenged by them, and continuingly guided by them.

The words and ways of our parents similarly outlive them, if they were wise and caring, and we have from them a challenge and an enduring wisdom. They continue in their work as parents. And in the other direction, a child who dies can never be forgotten by his or her parents. While their care may have no work to do, no way to embody its love, the love is there and the parenting goes on.

I came to see that during the years when children are young, when they are most visibly growing, when there are changes to behold every time you see them, it is really the parents who mature even faster than their children. In a household where children are being reared, the children make their parents come of age. It is possible that an infant may be leading his nursing mother out of youth faster than that mother can bring up the child. For parents the pace of growth may accelerate beyond anything they had experienced in their own youth.

## Children Change You Before They Arrive

If the bond between parents and children survives death, it also anticipates birth. When a couple make their decision to welcome a child, to leave themselves open to conception, that is when the child has his or her first and possibly most influential effect upon the parents. It is many years now since the late Pope Paul VI, severely troubled about family attitudes among Catholics, issued his letter *Humanae Vitae,* the best-known papal condemnation of contraception. There was much resistance to this message, much disbelief. It seemed to some of us, then and now, that the Holy Father's distinction between "artificial" and "natural" methods of birth control, which led him to classify the former as immoral, was inadequate. But resistance to that point obscured from most of the public the larger issue on which he was then taking a courageous and prophetic stand.

Beneath it all he sensed that in our time and especially in our Western world we have come, quietly and gradually, to have a distaste for children. Ours will not be known as an age which has welcomed children. The Pope spied something very pathological in our culture.

When you tie yourself to a person, you cannot control your future. Every one of us has within himself or herself an unbelievable potential for love and for generosity but we do not bring it out very willingly. It has to be drawn out of us. And the thing about marriage, as Christians understand it, is that the surprises encountered demand a love and generosity from us that we can in no way calculate or control. If that is so, then the incalculability of the demands of children fits very closely into the generosity that a man and a woman share in marriage. If a man and a woman can and do calculate and hedge the major claims made upon their generosity in the course of their marriage, then I fear that it is less a marriage of faith, and it will not blossom into a marriage of love such as Christians can enjoy.

Each new child that swells the brood can seem a burden: the loaf must now be sliced just that much thinner. Faith sees another side to it. Bread may be sliced thinner, but love is sliced larger, and greater love sets about winning more bread. Every person, every parent, is a fathomless well of love-potential. Children are not threats to love or competitors for it—they are new claims upon it, new tugs on the ungenerous heart to force it open further than it felt it could go. Children don't divide parents' love; they should invite it to multiply. Enormous resources of parent-love are let go stagnant in the heart's reservoirs for lack of children to make it gush and flow. Now obviously physical resources are not fathomless, and children must have bread. But in our age and culture, when parents feed their children cake and live in fear of a bread shortage, the Church weeps— and rightly so—that the children are starving in a famine of love.

A young woman at whose marriage I had officiated came to me several months later to tell me that every night during intercourse she was seized with fear she might conceive. They couldn't possibly, she cried, afford a baby yet. Knowing that her parents had given them a house and land, and that both husband and wife were working for good wages, I was rather surprised. As it turned out, they had gone heavily into debt to buy an oak living-room suite, a maple bedroom set, a mahogany dining room ensemble, a kitchen full of appliances, and complete laundry equipment—many thousands of dollars of furnishings. The unfortunate couple had been sold a bill of goods—not by the furniture salesman, but by the wacky culture which had persuaded them that a child came just below laundry equipment on their list of needs.

It was not that both spouses were working—many families have no choice. And even when there is a choice, both may have good reasons why they want to work. The problem this couple had—and many others too—is that they had never thought of themselves as a family and integrated their home life and their parenthood with their jobs. They were amassing at the very start the house and cars and furniture and clothing that their parents had taken years to acquire, and they put off for years the childbearing that had given satisfaction to the early years of their parents' marriage. Even when fully furnished their home was incomplete, because it still had no room for children.

My distress is that our quibbling over method fails to challenge the illusory motives which lead so many families to adopt contraception. This appears to be the case with individual couples, as also with entire peoples. In this country, for example, millions of families are pressed by medical urgency or financial crisis or similarly serious burdens that contraception can rightly relieve. And in numerous homes,

births are timed to allow either for further self-growth in
education, or for alternative forms of neighbor-service. But
I would estimate that far more couples avoid or curtail children because they share the grudging national attitude that
resents children as so many more drains on their generosity
and budget. Bluntly: selfishness is perhaps the most frequent excuse for contraception in this rich country. In this
regard, one would fault Pope Paul for having said too little,
rather than too much.

A readiness to accept children has traditionally been
thought to form part of the marriage promises. Just as a
nest is unfinished until shaped to the eggs and new-hatched
birds, so the home is yet immature until it has been shaped
to receive others besides the husband and the wife. A child
is felt even before the child is there. The tradition suspects
that you are hardly ready for sex until you can bear to have
children.

## Every Home Needs Rearranging

In a wedding ceremony the priest presiding puts to the
couple a series of questions, before the congregation as witnesses. A colleague of mine usually includes the following
question: "Are you willing to receive strangers into the hospitality of your home . . . and especially the strangers who
will come to you as your children?" It is a moving question,
and a wise one. Children do always arrive as strangers, with
personalities well on the way, and lives of their own to live.

Some people believe that there is a great difference
between your kinfolk and strangers. Your relatives, your
kinfolk, your family are the people who are always at home

in your home. They are the people who can take your commitment to them for granted. They belong to you, no matter what. They are the people, as Robert Frost says, who know that when they come to you, you have to take them in. Strangers, on the other hand, cannot know in advance whether they will find a welcome or a bolted door. Many people have said that the good thing about marriage is that it helps people, who would otherwise be unprepared, to open their hearts and homes to anyone: at least to take under their care and responsibility certain other persons.

But that says too little. Those on the inside should eventually come to realize that they are truly secure only if they live in a household that welcomes strangers. Young children are usually jealous of their parents' attention, and feel themselves rivaled by a new brother or sister, or by anyone to whom the parents give continuing attention. That feeling must eventually give way to greater wisdom.

I was reminded of this by *The Godfather*. The background of the story, according to author Mario Puzo, is the exploitation of Sicilian country-folk by a succession of foreign invaders. To protect themselves they eventually formed the Mafia, an intensely loyal fellowship of the poor who drew together in a defensive circle. The outer perimeter was maintained by the "soldiers," who used whatever violence was needed to protect their innocent women and children, who had no part in the bloodshed necessary to give them a peaceful life at the center. When the Sicilians came to this country, they found other people ready to take advantage of them, and so once again they erected the defensive perimeter for the sake of the innocent people at the center. In the story the wife of the Don was a daily communicant who presided over a household with almost no notice of the warfare that swirled around it.

But the flaw in the myth showed through in the very last scene of the film. Kay, who is Michael's young wife, and has become a Catholic and replaced her mother-in-law at the quiet center of the family, has asked Michael whether he was responsible for the murder of his brother-in-law. Michael says he was not; she leaves his room, knowing that he has lied to her. When she accepts that lie, you know, as he closes the door in the final dissolve, that there can no longer be innocence at the center because these apparently uninvolved people do know and accept the violence that guarantees them a perverse kind of peace.

It must be an uneasy peace for a home that raises children by killing parents in other homes. And no child can be truly secure in the hands of parents whose care for him or her is purchased by the neglect of other people's children.

Something of the same emerges from a study of couples who had a test given to their unborn children suspected of genetic handicaps. All agreed in advance that any unborn found to be injured would be eliminated. They were affluent whites, and this made a difference. Their experiences with handicapped children persuaded them that these youngsters led "unfulfilled lives." They wanted their children to have high health and intelligence, which their life-style required for a sense of adequacy and success. Most believed that abortion was destroying a life, but it was a life they would not welcome into their home. "These days you have a choice about having a baby," one mother explained. Another said: "The world has enough problems. I don't want to add to them." In general, the couples stood ready to abort for one common reason: to avoid hardship or misery for themselves.

How would these couples tell their healthy children that they would have been destroyed if imperfect? How would they tell an older, handicapped child that they had contemplated abortion rather than have another like him or her? One mother knew that an already affected child felt threatened by her visit to the center when she found him hiding in the closet upon returning. One father admitted that there was "no good way to explain to your own child that you might have had a part in deciding the end of his life."

The only home which is safe for anyone to be born into is the home that is ready to welcome someone who does not belong there by right of kinship, but belongs there in virtue of hospitality. A German student who was a house-guest in this country once taught me a lesson about hospitality. He said that in his country, a guest would be asked what his favorite foods and entertainments were, so that the family could supply them. But in American homes families thought themselves most hospitable if they said: "Make yourself at home. We're not going to make any fuss or do anything differently. We want you to feel like one of the family." Try as he would, he could not feel that a family which made no rearrangements was really welcoming him.

A household which makes room for a newcomer that is its own flesh and blood might learn that there are no strangers left in the world: that everyone out there is our sister and our brother, that other people's children are as important to us as our own. It is our own who bring us this sense of stewardship for the others. Care for our own children heightens our awareness of how many others need welcome and shelter. Our children teach us hospitality by being its first beneficiaries, but not its last or only ones.

Most of us are aware today of what autistic children are. We don't know very much about autism, but we do know that whether because of some terrible early rejection or because of some genetic disablement, a child can withdraw into herself or himself in remote and unreachable silence.

There are autistic parents too. Those who are unable or unwilling to provide the welcome in their homes which I have been trying to describe—for their own and for other people's children—are surely autistic parents, whether they refuse to have any children in the first place, or expect so much satisfaction from children that they neglect and abuse them when frustrated. These adults have drawn into their own remote interior, and so drastically cut themselves off that they cannot enter any further learning. An autistic child cannot be taught anything until he or she is somehow lured out of fear by love. It is probably true that there are husbands and wives who cannot receive any of the further gifts that marriage has to offer until they have been lured out of fear into love, love that opens their homes and lives to strangers. It is frightening that the first test, the one upon which all further progress depends, is such an awesome one: a readiness to hold someone else's entire life and character and eternity in one's arms. So great a lesson does a child have to teach, and so early.

## Not Playing Favorites

It is much easier to like people than to love them. We find it rather easy to appreciate those people who appeal to us, whom we find attractive. We say that those are the people we love, and we say sadly that there are other people we love less: in fact we find some hard to love at all. But that is a self-deception. Love is not the same as preference. Truly to love, we must embrace others not only for what we find attractive in them, but simply because we are committed to be good to them. It is not the goodness in them which links us together: it must also be the goodness in us.

As children, we need our parents to help us learn love: not simply to turn to others when we want something from them, but to give ourselves to others when apparently we have nothing to gain from it. In the parable of the prodigal son, the father is frustrated by each of his sons: one a runaway who had impoverished the family; the other, the kind of son every mother wanted to have. The story is not really about the son who runs away and finally comes home looking for work. It is about the father who fails to convince the younger son that he loves him and welcomes him home as a son, not as an employee. He loves him because he is his son. He fails to convince the other son who had so energetically supported him over the years that he loves him, not for his loyalty, but because he is his son. Neither son is mature enough to understand what the father is trying so hard to tell them both: that he loves the one who has not served and he loves the one who has served, and he loves them both in the same way. This ability to love other people generously and unselfishly is something we have to learn from our parents. It is also something that we as children have taught our parents. For it is with children that parents learn to give up favoritism.

Most parents have distinct preferences among their children. They will rarely say so, and perhaps they shouldn't say so, even to their spouses. Parents with twins face this in a particular way, but it is the same with all children. All parents—all persons—lead their lives by preference. We cross the street to greet a friend, and to avoid someone we find repulsive. We turn to greet the person we find attractive, and to ignore the bore. We write to those we wish to hear from; we postpone answering those who hold no similar appeal. And the more we treat others according to our likes and dislikes, the less likely it is that we shall grow in love. And it is children that can teach us to love without playing favorites.

## Learning To Be Aware

Christian churches do not agree about the proper age for baptism. The New Testament identifies baptism with moral transformation, faith, commitment and active membership in the community. Some churches therefore cannot accept the baptism of infants, since they are too young to act on their own. Better, they say, to wait until youngsters are old enough to speak for themselves.

The Catholic Church has continued the ancient practice of infant baptism, and there is in that practice an ancient wisdom. When we share with children the treasures we regard as most precious, we don't wait until our gifts can be perfectly understood. A youngster may need to grow into adulthood before he or she gains a proper sense of what it is to be honest; but that doesn't mean we should hesitate until the youngster's eighteenth birthday to begin teaching him or her not to lie. In fact, the greater gifts in life are not the gifts we asked for, but the gifts that were beyond our appreciation, which wiser people gave us, and which made us grow in order to possess them. If I ask for a bicycle, what

I get leaves me delighted but unchanged. But if I am given suffering, or learning, or courtesy, none of which I asked for, these are things which enlarge me.

It is the larger gifts, the ones that are unrequested because we don't yet know we need them, which provoke us to grow high enough to handle them. And these are the gifts which parents owe their children. Not only must they be generous: they must anticipate what the children need. This calls for a sort of providential care, a readiness to foresee the best course for a child's path to take. One must grow to be preoccupied with the child, for one's gifts need to be guided by one's own wisdom. To do this we have to extend ourselves in a way we generally don't have to do for fellow adults who can know and make known their needs.

This is symbolized well by what I like to call "mothers' ears." When you are at a crowded house party, and everyone is shouting and partying and no one is listening, all of a sudden the mother of the house will exclaim, "Oh, the baby!" No one else could hear a thing, least of all the father. But the mother, with that sense mothers develop, hears the thin peep of the child crying. It is almost like a dog whistle: the mother can hear a frequency which others miss. I use this only as a symbol: a symbol of an attentiveness that none of us is born with. It is a providential, intense care for someone else, a readiness to foresee and to ponder in advance what another human being needs, an imaginative effort to put as much mental energy into someone else's future needs as into your own. That does not come easily: to be so preoccupied with someone else. It is one of the great gifts—not entirely anticipated or asked for—which the child brings to his or her parents.

## Fully Feminine, Maturely Masculine

Carl Gustav Jung has pointed out that none of us is purely male or female. The doctors have already told us that we have both sets of hormones and perhaps even both sets of organs, but one kind is dominant while the other is recessive, or vestigial. Jung refers to the *animus* and the *anima:* the masculine and feminine soul, or principle. All of us, whatever our gender, need a touch of the opposite gender to round out our makeup. Adolescence is a time when most of us work particularly hard to define ourselves as men or women, to develop and even accentuate our femininity or masculinity. Courtship, and the early time of marriage before childbearing, are times when this gender-definition is most intense, when gender traits are strongly reinforced, and formed against the companionship and intimacy of a partner of the opposite sex. So much conspires then to make a person operatively male or female.

But when children come a new arrangement is possible. One can see that fathers become more tender than mere husbands, and mothers become a little more decisive than mere wives. In raising both sons and daughters, men and women come to understand and to accommodate the emerging features of male and female. A woman might learn more about masculinity, and about getting along with males, from her young sons than even from her husband. Children help us fill out our gender, to shade in our masculinity or femininity, to write the accompaniment into the score.

## Giving Children Privacy

As children move into adolescence they have to be addressed with greater distance, respect and understanding.

A marriage begins when a husband and wife share their privacies with one another. That is a sharing meant to last their lifetime. But children born into that privacy must not be imprisoned there. They must be given a privacy of their own, so that they may eventually go forth and offer it sensibly to someone else. They have to be allowed to draw apart from their parents. During adolescence it again becomes clear that these are people the parents have poured their lives into, only to see them start to go their own ways. It is a difficult thing to see how much of your life you have spent for your children, and to know that you are not going to possess them.

At that time, just as children are beginning to withdraw they demand that their parents reveal more of themselves. Just when the children are getting very private about themselves they start to make more and more challenges to the parents' privacy. For example, why is it that most parents admit their failure in telling their children the facts of life? Almost anyone could explain the plumbing involved. There are atrocious books and films and courses in some schools that people imagine to be giving sex education without ever ranging beyond the physical details. But they aren't. The reason that parents, despite their own failures, get very nervous about public servants giving sex education is that real sex education requires an ethic, a vision of values. For parents to do justice by their children in this matter, they would have to tell them the story of their own love life, their closest relations. Those are the real facts of life: how they have struggled over the years, sometimes faltering and sometimes succeeding, to become two-in-one. Imagine having to tell that to your child just at the point when the child doesn't want to tell you anything. Children in adolescence require, even though they do not often have it themselves, considerable maturity and unselfishness. They offer their parents no immediate prospect of payoff. All efforts may prove to have been in vain. You still have to do it. They require a more advanced and mature type of unselfishness.

The closer children approach adulthood, the more stressful it is for parents. I do not refer to that endocrine-based, temporary insanity which teenagers experience, but to something else. On our campus, most seniors within two or three weeks of graduation finally arrive at the point where they know which courses one should take in college. In the same way, it is just when their children are moving off into their own unsupervised ventures that parents have figured out what parenting is all about. Just when their children are moving beyond arm's length, and are slipping out of their grasp, parents become most aware of how incomplete their work has been, what their shortcomings were, what maturing urgently requires still to be done.

What children do not seem to know, particularly at that age, is that most men and women judge the success of their marriage—indeed, of their life—by how their children turn out. They feel particularly helpless exactly when they become aware of this, and just when they can no longer have much say in how the children are going to turn out. A parent's life is in a child's hands.

This is also when parents have to understand that their children are not simply the sum of their efforts, but have a character and a will and a course of their own ... and a responsibility too. Their children sin. They stumble and fall. They have faults, richly developed faults. At this point there is the temptation to give and take blame: "Where did we go wrong?" (Or: "Where did *you* go wrong?") This very temptation to blame oneself is often another form of the need to possess the child, to refuse to give him or her any self-responsibility. It can be a denial of the fact that parents really hold their children in trust for a very brief spell.

Children mean more to parents than parents mean to children, when both are young. At the age when children are leaving, they are looking forward to *their* education, *their* career, *their* friends, *their* decisions, *their* family, where *they* are going to live. They are beginning to be grateful, very grateful, for the advantages their parents have given them, but they seem to remember their parents only on very special occasions. They feel less and less limited by the faults of their parents.

But the parents, who might appear to be looking forward to their own freedom and a life together unburdened by children—the parents are looking at the children. They judge themselves by those children. And they have to go through the harder sacrifice of not trying to possess the children, and not doing a post-mortem on everything they did as parents. They must accept that they made mistakes, as all do, and that they will simply have to be forgiven for those mistakes, whose results they will continue to see in their children. Those mistakes can be redeemed now, but only by personal transformation in the children. Those are not things that are easy to learn. But one hasn't grown up until one has learned them.

Parents are probably more challenged when their children become adults, and most challenged when their children have children. It is not that their children are now their equals, and know everything that *they* know. They don't. In fact, it is very clear that they don't, at least to the grandparents. Parents who have just learned what child-rearing is all about, when their youngest children are going out the door, now have to become master teachers. They must now pass on their wisdom without being in physical control. They have to persuade, not so much by what they say as by what they do. They really always did need to persuade, but now it is clearer that they do. On the other hand, now they are able to tell tales on themselves. Now they don't always need to appear so strong and faultless. Indeed, one of the best ways grandparents teach parents is by telling them the stories of their own colossal mistakes. It is a humble time.

It is possible that the bond between parents and children is strongest at this time. That means that the ideal family picture is not of a pair of parents in their thirties, with one child about ten and another seven years old. The portrait should include a couple with two or perhaps three children in their thirties, and their spouses, and a scatter of grandchildren from infancy up through elementary years. It is our loss that we do not picture a family this way, in its fullness and maturity.

## When Your Children Have Children

Arthur Kornhaber and Ken Woodward's excellent book *Grandparents/Grandchildren: The Vital Connection* points out that grandparents can help parents understand better than ever before that they are stewards and not owners of their children. They even have to share their grandchildren with other grandparents. My father, when my brother began presenting him with a procession of grandchildren, was unnerved by the need to share them with another grandfather, whom he persisted in calling "Brand X."

From grandparents, parents can begin to learn that by themselves they are insufficient to the task of rearing children. We know that a single-parent home faces a great handicap. But it is an older insight that a double-parent home also operates under a handicap. No two people are enough to raise a child. Grandparents can finally realize what earlier in life they could not have accepted so easily: that they can continue to give of themselves more and more freely to youngsters who are their own, and then more and more let that generosity overflow to other youngsters who are not their own . . . and yet, who are.

# 5    *The Implausible Promise*

Many people are surprised that marital promises are so frequently spoken to the wind. The statistics are known: more than a third of all American marriages now end in divorce; about a third of those people now marrying are survivors of divorce and are entering unions with an even higher break-up rate than their earlier marriages. My surprise, however, is otherwise: I wonder why there are not more divorces.

As a Catholic, I am warned by our tradition that marriage is the most dangerous thing that ordinary people do. Just when a person has become independent of home and family, and has developed and understood one's personal appetites and interests, and has dreamed one's dreams— just then, he or she surrenders that independence. No one is ready to marry until he or she has somehow asserted himself or herself as free from family; but just then, one is expected to give up that freedom, to live at one with another person who has till then been developing her or his own individuality. How could anyone imagine that this kind of undertaking would be successful?

Our tradition also tells me that there is no affection nor compatibility nor ecstasy between man and woman that can make them two-in-one, or can help them grow together;

steadfast loyalty and service, though, *can* make them one and can summon up the affection that makes the oneness joyful. It also teaches that marriage will be followed by a succession of other calls to other cubits of self-growth through self-giving.

No sooner do a man and a woman settle into a rhythm of companionship than it is disturbed by crying in the night, and burdened by a perpetual papoose. More to live, more to love.

No sooner has a child grown to hear, to obey, to go potty properly, than another arrives, a beginner in the process parents had just figured out: a rookie at childhood just when they are all stars in motherhood and fatherhood. More to live, more to love.

No sooner have the children grown to make something of themselves, with orthodontists and adolescence and zits all left behind, than they want to leave their parents behind too, and their eyes and minds look other places for fun and future and the sharing of confidences. More to live, more to love.

No sooner has career experience risen to a point where one could now take on much higher responsibilities, than one discovers that the years of climb are over, and one must make do with other kinds of satisfaction. More to live, more to love.

No sooner are wives and husbands freed of their full household, and ready for the quieter times for reacquaintance (strong enough now to accept that one's lifelong partner is not as stimulating as one might have hoped, and now not so likely any more to rejuvenate), than there comes the spoilage of illness and the evening of energy. More to live, more to love.

And, amid all those common changes in the seasons of marriage, there come the squalls, the unexpected strokes: a daughter arrived home with her child, an uncongenial in-law to take in, a wife's romance, a husband fired from his work, a young widowing, a child lost to drugs or highway accident, a son-in-law whose eye cannot meet yours. More to live, more to love.

Always more. Never enough. Always to stretch, to accommodate, to put away preference. The energies and wisdom and patience needed for the last tough time never seem enough for the next. More growth always seems to be required, simply to be able to continue on. And this is if one is lucky and supported, not thwarted. If your partner is at this particular time an added burden, not a comrade, then you feel ready to break.

It is astonishing, then, that more men and more women do not give up and abandon their marital commitments. If marriage requires of a person such a continual sacrifice of self to common needs—and this sometimes when one's partner is at fault—then instead of asking "How do so few fail?" we should simply say, "If that is how things are between husband and wife, it is not advisable to marry."

Does this sound like cynicism? It may sound strange and inappropriate from within a tradition which seems to teach that marriage for better, for worse, until death is as available to most people as, say, balancing one's checkbook stubs, or driving with a stick-shift, or stopping the greasies.

But that is not what our tradition tries to convey. Fidelity in marriage, it teaches, is about as easy as being a cheerful paraplegic, or recovering from alcoholism, or forgiving an associate who has embezzled you into bankruptcy. To give one's life away to a lifelong partner, and to go on growing and coping and forgiving faithfully enough to have it endure as long as promised: that, our tradition teaches, is extraordinary, not ordinary.

But it is no more extraordinary, no stronger, no more dangerous, no more difficult, than fidelity to God. The promises of Christian faith are struck at the same mint as the promises of Christian marriage: both promise to persevere for better or for worse throughout an unknown future; both volunteer for missions through territory sometimes friendly, sometimes hostile; both survive only by repeated forgiving, a forgiveness pledged before the offense. Christians believe about marriage what we believe about faith: that bones are often broken when humans collide, but the healed bone is strongest at the mend.

So infidelity to marriage vows should be no more or less astonishing than infidelity to baptismal vows, or any other abandonment of others when the cost of faithfulness is felt.

## Special Strains on Marriages Today

Perhaps it will become worse than it is now. One thing to worry about is that the current change in the public and social relationships between men and women may possibly provoke even more disintegration of marriage and family.

This is not to imply that in the past we have had male-female patterns which were all that nourishing to family. Sometimes they have starved it.

For instance, we all know this pattern. After their marriage, the young wife supports her young husband in his dedication to excel. Through long working hours and evenings on the job and weekends devoted to the job, he manages to rise within his career. There is travel, perhaps, and certainly preoccupation and fatigue, as the price of his ambition. She is left as sole maintainer of the home to bear and raise the children, to cater when he presides at table, to soothe him when he comes to rest. He is ill at ease about his children: they do not find the time to eat or vacation or study or play together much. She is vaguely disappointed about the loneliness of her motherhood, and occasionally angry that the family, which when younger seemed simpler and closer-bound and more at home, has had to pay such a price for her husband's success. When the last child moves out, she is left alone in a vacant house and an empty life. He, for his part, now finds her company boring, and no relief for his weariness. She has, in fact, aged more rapidly than he has, and she takes less womanly interest in him than do other females who seem to take him less for granted. Usually it is her anger rather than his distraction which seeks out a lawyer and divorce, after decades of marriage.

The pattern is one we all know, including those of us who teach the child survivors of such families. It is unhealthy from the start, I think. It is a household built across a seismic fault: husband absent from the home and wife confined to it. The trouble does not arise when a husband and wife allot out the breadwinning and the housekeeping as need or wish or custom might suggest. The trouble arises when a primary responsibility for one of these sectors is corrupted into a possessive hold on it. It is one thing for a man to work, quite another for him to excuse himself from his home. It is one thing for a wife to be a homemaker, quite another for her to have to be a twenty-four-hour sentry there. Choosing the marketplace or the household is not what pries partners apart. That is done when either task is relished or relinquished for itself alone, more than for the family, for the home; not as a recognition of appropriate sex roles, but as a defense of psychological separation.

A marriage can fall apart in a million ways. In the disaster I have described, ordinary human foolishness is aggravated by popular prejudices about how men and women should live together. There are other patterns, too, as when the man fails to support his wife and children and forces her to be both breadwinner and homemaker, or when the woman joins the man as full-time careerist and they leave the children to fend for themselves.

Those are all patterns we have become used to. But another pattern is lately emerging which strikes me as new and sad and likely to increase.

A young man and a young woman are attracted to one another and marry. He is at the start of his career. He means to stand highest among his workmates, and determines not to let anything stand between him and excellence. She supports him. When he is in professional training she supports them both. When he must move to follow opportunity, it is she who packs and moves and sets up house accordingly: one, two or ten times. When he is exhausted from his work, she is there to revive him. When they bring forth children together she nests them, watches them, is both mother and father to them.

It is, after all, an old pattern. She had grown, like other girls, to accommodate to boys. The boys were on the field, competing with each other; the girls were cheerleaders on the sidelines. She grew to be the ivy on his wall. She shaped herself to him and to his interests. It was not so much that he beckoned and she followed, as that he went about his business knowing she would be there beside him. There had come to be an inequality between them, but it was one to which she gave her consent.

Everything between them, as I say, is without complaints. None, that is, until lately, when their lopsided union is shaken by a few spasms. There comes a day when, her husband well into his career, she undertakes some venture on her own. He delights in this, and encourages her to give her homebound life some outside opportunity. She might do some freelance writing. Or finish up her interrupted college work. Or lend a hand in precinct politics. Or start the long haul towards a law degree, or even a medical one. Or take on a local agency for battered children, or refugees, or the retarded. Or assume the management of a small business. What makes her different from previous women who reactivated themselves as teachers, nurses, secretaries and librarians is that she is venturing into something with climb in it, and an opportunity to ascend: something no longer acquiescent.

She does advance. After a while she is asked to run for the school board. Or she is wanted as a consultant. Or she chairs the committee she just joined. Or she is invited into a business partnership. Things happen then. It may not be as exhausting as her husband's work, but it does lead her to rearrange her home life. More day care for the children; more crockpot dinners and fewer ironed shirts; a thin film of dust has begun to settle around the house, and there is a touch less of gentle warmth for her husband in his wearier moments, less time to listen to his war-stories.

After a while her husband begins to feel that she is neglecting her family duties. And now she is often tired, short-tempered and preoccupied. He asks about all this and suggests that she has let her enjoyment draw her from her greater commitments. She hears. But it doesn't work so well. Her appetites have been aroused, and her abilities are more and more demanded by those she works with.

Finally he complains. She is letting him down, neglecting their marriage and family for her own selfish pursuit of a career. At this point—usually for the first time—she begins her slow burn. Who says his work is always dutiful while hers is her private enjoyment? Who says that his fixation on career and his estrangement from their children are virtuous, while she is run to a frazzle to keep him comforted, to keep the home fires burning, to do some honest service in the world—and then called self-indulgent? Why, after having supported him full-time for so many years, must she be put on the defensive about doing some part-time work as an adult with adults? Who says she is the disrupter?

And so, to protect her small amount of freedom, she ignores him. His accusation then becomes self-fulfilling. He had called her selfish, and now in her annoyance she uses the only weapon at hand: her selfishness. Her ego toughens up and sharpens its wits. Contention within the home and competition outside both toughen her. She develops a sharp eye for turf and boundaries; she will not give up yardage if it is not paid for. She, her husband's long-time confidante, now finds friends to counsel her, female friends who tell her how justice comes to those who hustle for it, in the home and out.

Although he cannot really put his finger on it, he is disconcerted by her transformation. From youngest manhood he had somehow been habituated to being in charge. He stood higher in his shoes than women did. He had had the edge of age. He moved more easily in the world's affairs. His schooling was more carefully provided. His was the major income, his the savvy, his the brunt of ego-batting in the marketplace. His women, his woman, were always weaker than he. If they were really brighter or quicker or more resolute, they made their contributions deftly—by habit, and by a primitive sense that men don't seem to want intimacy with women who can compete with them eye-to-eye.

This man is now bewildered by his wife who is not the woman he had married. She is challenging, not trusting. She has gristle where she once was gentle. He becomes peevish, hurt, sullen, even childish at times. She comes into a sort of strength; he retreats into weakness. Neither is becoming.

In fact, he had been selfish from the start. And she had been pretty selfish to marry him. It may appear that she had been generous and devoted for all those years, and then changed into a woman who was out for herself. But that is a shallow view of it all. It is never generous to humor a partner who is ungenerous.

Had this man been truly generous and this woman been truly resolute from the start, their life together would have followed a different course. But like everyone else they came to a point where their own deficiencies and their own life choices gave them only two options. They could outgrow their faults or they could get worse.

I expect that much good is going to come of the enormous renegotiation now underway between men and women, about their roles in our world. It could bring new freedom and honesty to many, and could rid many homes of exploitation. But at the moment it is a painful and threatening social change. It forces many men and women to re-embrace in the aftermath of unanticipated changes. For the few who knew that they had promised to forgive every fault and every meanness, to be faithful to their partners no matter how they were transformed, the great shifts that now unsettle their partnerships strain them to the breaking point. For those many more who never heard of such promises, and who took as their mates the persons who they thought stood before them, with no readiness or promises for the strange persons those mates might later become—for those, the strains are overwhelming.

The issue is not how much time, energy and attention either partner gives to the home or to work. Younger couples have found increasingly that the model of the invisible father and the imprisoned mother can be improved on. What both partners need is enough strength of character so that neither will take advantage (or be allowed to take advantage) of the other, and enough generosity that they do not both slight their children.

What I see now, in all this shifting around, is women scrambling for the same unhealthy career addictions that entrapped men. What I hope to see in time is a rededication of both men and women to home and hearth and to life-giving there, as a protected household from which husband, wife and children can, with mutual encouragement, go out to do the work they want and the world needs.

## A Single Message on Marriage—For All

In the meantime we have to step through the wreckage of massive divorce. As a churchman, a student of and a spokesman for a tradition I regard as wise, I ask myself what we as a Christian community can do to be of more help than we now are. There are two things I would like to see our Church accomplish in the face of widespread divorce: to ensure that its many services to families coordinate their deeds and messages, and to reassert the value and possibilities of Jesus' marriage promises.

The typical Catholic diocese in this country is as diversified a resource agency for families as one can find. The marriage preparation program, working through the parishes, usually sponsors Pre-Cana workshops, weekends or Engagement Encounter sessions for couples intending to marry. Married couples are served by the Christian Family Movement, by Cana or similar discussion groups, or by Marriage Encounters. Through Catholic hospitals pregnant couples are readied for natural childbirth; groups also exist now for those who anticipate cesarean delivery. Natural family planning groups are also widespread. Families who want to welcome other children are helped by the adoption bureaus of Catholic Charities. Support for unmarried women with distressful pregnancies is offered in virtually every diocese, along with pre-natal and post-natal care and counseling. Couples in difficulty can usually find professional counseling available in the Family Life Office or Catholic Social Services. Homes in a financial emergency can usually receive funding for utility bills, food or clothing quicker and with fewer questions asked from St. Vincent de Paul or Catholic Charities than from regulated government agencies. Families with special needs, such as the elderly or refugees or Spanish-speaking, or with handicapped children, are served by concerned agencies in the average diocese. Marriage tribunals exist to try to reconcile estranged couples or to inquire into the original validity of their marriage bond. Sympathetic ministry to separated and divorced Catholics is now going on throughout the country.

The scope of family services offered under Catholic auspices in each region is impressive. If there is improvement to be made, it might be through a higher consistency of purpose. Some fear that in one office, the marriage tribunal, annulments are being issued much too easily. When a diocese issues, for example, 697 annulments out of 700 cases filed, often to couples who have lived together to see their children's children, one wonders if these are not simply divorces in the disguise of annulments. Meanwhile, on the other side of the chancery office, the Pre-Cana program may be processing for marriage youngsters who, to a trained eye, are ideal candidates for annulment in years to come. Those who work with the elderly gain an experience and a wisdom that might sober the discussions of the couples working out their childbearing preferences.

I fear that the people who offer these various services tend to operate from different perspectives. Those who work with the romantic young often become as naively optimistic as their clientele. Meanwhile, their colleagues who sift through the human wreckage of damaged families find it difficult not to acquire the habits of mind of a bankruptcy judge. The family counseling staff may be operating on values which are in conflict with those that the family planning people are offering.

The Church, as I understand it, has a hopelessly (and hopefully) complex teaching on marriage, blending promise and pragmatism, covenant and forgiveness, welcome for children and accent on adulthood. The various aspects of this wholeness will be emphasized differently in different operations of the Church. But when these services go by their separate paths in diverging directions, the young are too often indulged and not sobered; those in difficulty are too often given sympathy without challenge.

I would like to see all the family-related operations of a local church in touch with one another. Let the annulment people go over the Pre-Cana program for the engaged so that it does not simply repeat known mistakes. The ministry to the separated and divorced should have to satisfy those working with newlyweds. Adopting procedures should be reviewed by marriage counselors. The St. Vincent de Paul people and the staffers of the school program for unwed mothers should work in harmony with one another, and both should join with the handicapped and refugee offices in leaning on the diocesan schools. The initiative of the various agencies might possibly be weakened by bureaucratic control under a single administration, but at least all the parties should be locked up together periodically to account for their work and their principles to one another—and not let out until they agree that every facet of the mysterious Christian tradition of marriage is seen in every one of the services they offer.

A second suggestion for the Church arises from what I call the predominance of pathology. Let me illustrate this by a medical comparison. Many doctors know little and care little about health. They are trained and sought out and paid to take care of disorders and dysfunction and disease. A doctor is presented with a broken clavicle, not a sound one. He is more interested in an endocrine imbalance than in normalcy. Apart from non-medical functions which some doctors perform on the healthy, like cosmetic implants and abortions, medical professionals are by training and by instinct concerned to remedy pathologies. Even this professional concern seems to evaporate when they cannot relieve the problem as, for example, when a child is chronically hanicapped or an adult is terminally ill. Most doctors are wiser about treating disease than about cultivating health. This is what I call the predominance of pathology.

In the Church today the most articulate voices being raised are commenting on marital breakdown. Counselors point out that the crushing strains imposed by an unsympathetic society make marital happiness almost impossible. There is much study of the hazards to growing children created in many homes. Tribunal officials argue that many marriages have begun with flimsy and inattentive motivation (admitting that no one can foresee all the consequences of open-ended vows). What they say seems supported by the evidence.

But those observations need balancing by others. The Christian tradition preserved most tenaciously in the Catholic communion is that Jesus came to call sinners. His call was to purge ourselves of self-preference, to spend ourselves on our neighbor's needs, to pledge our lives and energies and possessions to the Lord through the service of those whom we acknowledge as beloved brothers, sisters, neighbors.

Jesus also calls those who wed to pledge their lives and energies and possessions to each other, for better, for worse, come what may, till death. He acknowledged that to make such pledges was apparently ridiculous, because of human fault and frailty—but grandly possible by God's strength breathed into our weakness. And he also called wives and husbands to share their lives and substance with children, for better, for worse, come what may, till death. Another folly made divinely possible.

Christians have no specific wisdom regarding the disintegration of marriage and family. We do, however, have astounding and peculiar beliefs about what makes marrying and childbearing endure. Perhaps I speak from my bias as an educator, but the best way to prevent divorce in our time seems to be to prevent frivolous or selfish marriages at the outset. I respect those who believe that some husbands or wives cannot realistically be expected to fulfill their marital commitments, or that some of these commitments were handicapped from the beginning. But our message and our conviction are that common men and common women, by God's grace, can marry and beget and

make household together in the teeth of failures and immaturity and even infidelity. I do not want our sad recognition
of marital pathology to cloud over our joyful appreciation
of marital health. The Church's ministry to marriage is not
that of a coroner.

What we say to the most battered marriage veteran we
say to the most bright-eyed adolescent in love. For each, joy
will come at the cost of some suffering. In fact, our tradition
has usually been thought insensitive because it spoke of
sorrow to the optimists, while reminding pessimists of their
promises. To the youngsters at the altar we speak of adultery, the trials of children, poverty and death. To the dis-
couraged and estranged we speak of the hopes of their
youth, and of enduring, and of reconstructing the ruins.

At this time of epidemic divorce, of the scorning of
marriage and the abandonment of children, of disbelief in
fidelity to pledges or in devotion stubborn enough to yield
joy—precisely at this time we should shout that the way of
marriage is the way of survival, that the most certain thing
we know is to undertake what is least certain, that tenacity
until death defies and defeats death. It is the look in the
eyes of Jesus crucified.

Our reaction to divorce is not to deny it but both to
prevent it and to survive it. Knowing that many fail at marriage should not frighten us into lesser promising, lesser
risk, lesser hope. It should arouse us, though, to oppose the
sentimentality and self-indulgence and irresponsibility that
are drawing many young people today into pathetic marriages in which the risk is not the risk of giving away your
whole life to another, but the risk of pretending to give it

away when you have never yet gathered it into your own hands.

By reinforcing our faith in Jesus' strange and implausible promises we shall best serve both those who stand by them and those who have stumbled under them but need not be defeated.

**6** *When You Are*
*Ready for Marriage:*
*Some Thoughts on Weddings*

This book is intended to be of interest and of help to men and women who are thinking about marriage. Some people would naturally have matrimony on their minds because they are planning to get married soon. It is regrettable that for many in their position, concern for the wedding can eclipse concern for the marriage. They are not helped by some of the marriage preparation programs which often prepare them more for the wedding and less for the marriage.

Still, weddings are very important for the same simple reason that marriage and family are very important. And if your wedding is to ring true, you need to give it some thought and taste and attention. There are plenty of books and professional people that specialize in the protocol of weddings. They can be of use in suggesting meaningful ways to celebrate the beginning of your life together. Or you can put yourself in the hands of an expert with Amy Vanderbilt under the arm and a clipboard in hand, and be walked through your paces with MGM accuracy. What I offer here are some observations that may be of some help, but they will only be of use if a couple talk them over with each other and with the people they trust to create the celebration with them. What I have to suggest is the result of personal experiences, and may not be to everyone's taste.

The first and most important wedding preparation is a peaceful understanding with your family. If they are against your marriage, they are hardly going to enthuse about the wedding. But even if they are cheering you on, there are some important understandings you must arrive at.

There are precise expectations about who pays for what at weddings, down to the bridesmaids' shoes and the groom's cake. But most importantly, it has been traditional that the bride's parents pay for most wedding expenses. They were therefore the hosts for the occasion, and they naturally had most say in how the celebration was planned and carried out (in continuity with the even older tradition by which they also chose the groom).

Today many engaged persons have long since established a life for themselves outside their parental home. Some may even be better able than their parents to afford the wedding costs, and willing—even preferring—to do that. Sometimes the groom's parents are anxious to help with the expenses if the other family would not take it amiss. But it should be established very clearly, with dollar amounts specified as much as possible, who will contribute what.

Once upon a time that would also have determined who would decide on the arrangements, but today this has become a very separable matter. Parents and children may come with very different expectations: who makes the invitation lists, who hires the hall and picks the musicians, and so on. A marriage is no private matter: it is a public concern, and the community has a stake in it. A wedding is therefore a public celebration, where several families and their friends and the Church at large all have a stake in what the couple are doing with their lives. It is not their private affair, and it can become tense and awkward if all concerned do not share a settled plan about who is in charge of what. It is not usually helpful for two parties to have the say over any one item. But it is very wise to circulate your ideas provisionally for comments and suggestions before the decision is finally made. To illustrate: the bride's parents offer a total sum that they can contribute; this leads to the agreed estimate that two hundred guests can be invited; fifty of these invitations are allotted to the groom's parents to send to their family and friends, since it is they who live at a distance and will be less represented; the groom's parents pass their list by the bride and groom for any changes that they would recommend; the parents adjust the list and the invitations go out. Everyone was clear about who would make the decision, but others felt they had been heard. Many parties had a say without competing for final say-so.

Ancient custom prescribed that a woman was wedded by being brought by her father to her husband's house. Christian sentiment changed that. No matter who is actually present on the particular occasion, the Church at large is the witnessing and supporting community that gathers around a couple who declare they want to be faithful to each other as Jesus is faithful to us. Weddings, like Eucharists, found their way out of private homes into the halls where Christians assembled. The more recent custom has been for the bride's parish church to be the presumed place for the wedding. The pastors of each spouse have a responsibility to clear him or her for marriage, but if the couple have good reasons for wanting their wedding in another church that will have them (this could be for reasons of location or size or sentimental attachment) the pastors should agree to help them arrange for that.

People who never blink at having to reserve a band or a restaurant for their reception a year in advance can somehow take offense when they are informed that most local churches now expect six months' lead time for their wedding. Unlike the photographer or the bakery or the tuxedo rental shop, the Church has got to ready them for their married life, not just their wedding day. So it is difficult to take seriously a couple that sashays in to schedule their nuptials two or three weeks beforehand.

The pastor of the church where the wedding occurs is responsible to preside, but this role he can and often does delegate to one of his associates who knows the couple well, or to a priest or deacon from elsewhere who has some special tie to them. If there is a priest the couple would like to invite, it is up to them to clear this with the pastor, so that he can authorize the invitation. Occasionally there are several clergy the families wish to take part in the wedding. If they are numerous the ceremony can take on the look of a Wagnerian opera with too many spear-carriers. Even three priests can be a crowd, but if you want three you must make it perfectly clear to all of them who is the principal celebrant and chief witness, and whether there is another priest you would want to preach. Otherwise the clergy are left in the embarrassing position that whoever takes the initiative appears to be making a takeover bid. Or a priest is invited by the bride and groom to travel a few thousand miles to preside at their wedding, only to find that the local priest didn't have that understanding, and fully expects to be in the center chair.

Someone from the church will need to help you with certain of the wedding preparations. The priest who presides should plan the ceremony with you. Someone conveniently close to where you live—a priest or a layperson who regularly handles this responsibility for the parish—will draw up the important papers: certificates of baptism, affidavits that you are free to marry, interrogatories to establish your readiness for marriage, any dispensations that might be needed. Even if your wedding is being arranged in a parish far from where one or both are living, your local church will usually be cooperative in helping with the paperwork.

Much more importantly though, the Church will offer help in readying you for a lifetime of marriage and family. Catholics who lack initiation in Christian belief and practice will have access to a course of inquiry and instruction. Non-Catholics who will be partners of Catholics will also have an introduction to the teaching and tradition of the Church. And everyone who marries will be expected to join in one of the available programs of pre-marital reflection and discussion. In one format, the couple will join with a number of others at presentations by physicians, marriage counselors, clergy and married couples. Or they may spend an intensive weekend in an encounter hosted by a cadre of laypeople. Or, in yet another format, they may spend a series of evenings, two-on-two, with a veteran couple who share a candid account of how they have been meeting the challenges of a shared life. Whatever format is followed, the point of this preparation is to break through the distractions and excitement of engagement to confront a man and woman with the sober realities of what is facing them, and to lend them the encouragement of others who are ahead of them on the same road.

Engaged couples should not get the feeling that all this preparation is so much bureaucratic red-tape or an intrusion into their privacy. Marriage is not something they are about to create. It is a society they will join. It is only natural that the community's elders, who know that marital love has many counterfeits, should put challenging questions to them about precisely those things that are most personal: sex, wealth, jealousy, childbearing. It is the least they can do.

When a Catholic is marrying someone of another church, or of no church, his or her own community will naturally exhibit its concerns. Our hope is that the bond of marriage is reinforced by the bond of Christian faith and fellowship. When one takes a partner from outside this faith and fellowship the questions are serious but understandable. Does the non-Catholic partner understand his or her future partner's own faith and tradition well enough that it will not be a source of puzzlement or—worse—a cause for antagonism? To prevent this the Church offers to give an account of its faith and tradition to those coming close through marriage. Does the non-Catholic partner join in the intention to marry in Christ: for better or for worse, until death? To help bring this out in the open the Church asks both parties seriously if this is their resolve. Does the non-Catholic partner agree to leave the Catholic spouse free to share his or her faith with their children, insofar as one can ever pass on one's beliefs to one's children? To assure this beforehand, and not leave it as a hazy and avoided issue, the Church asks the non-Catholic partner to state his or her intentions. Even if faith is not there to reinforce the pledge between husband and wife, the Church believes that their marriage is much better off when it is established from the start that the marital partnership leaves full religious freedom to the Catholic party, as spouse and as parent.

The Catholic preference is to offer the hospitality of our churches to couples entering a mixed marriage. This is particularly so because of our tenacious hold on the belief that Christians have a distinctive promise to make when they marry. But it is possible for Catholics to be given leave by their own community to celebrate their marriages in the churches of their spouses. It is quite common for us to invite clergy close to the non-Catholic spouse to take an active part in our marriage rites, and to accept a reciprocal hospitality in other churches. This can be discussed with one's pastor beforehand.

If, by common agreement, the religious commitments of the wedding party and the congregation would be more divided than united by the celebration of the wedding inside the Eucharist, it is better to celebrate it by itself, though of course with the Scripture reading and sermon and blessings and singing that would otherwise have formed part of the rite. Communion is meant to bind people together, not separate them into factions.

In the Catholic tradition, the right moment for a man and woman to gives their lives away to each other is at Mass, when we are banqueting in memory of God's only Child who gave his life away that we might know the Father's heart. It is nothing you do off by yourselves. In fact, when you rise to this moment you are declaring to the community of Jesus-followers that you are now ready as an adult to advance toward the center of what the mystery means: the faith-mystery in which we lay down our lives only to take them up again, transfigured. At the Eucharist a man and a woman put down their lives as the earnest of their good faith. Their pledge to each other is their manifest display that they mean something when they make their pledges to the Lord.

When the Eucharist is the scene for a marriage feast it is doubly arrayed in custom and old sentiment. There is a paradox about these and similar traditions. They go stale unless you enter into them to the point where they are as much yours as if you had invented them. No couple invent marriage. It is a way of life that the community preserves as a tradition, and you enter into it, you don't invent it. The community—the Church in our case—even puts words in your mouth. You can either recite those words like a policeman reading to an arrested suspect his or her legal rights, or you can make them your own. One woman I know astonished her husband by turning to him at the wedding and singing her vows: her way of putting her whole self into their meaning.

A wedding is either encumbered or enriched by so many customary things to do and to say: rings and toasts and prayers and garters and invitations and veils and seating arrangements and honeymoons and thank-you cards and *tarantelle* and sexual consummation and portraits and handkerchiefs that had been worn as baptismal caps. All of these things have a history and a meaning. All of them mark the path that so many others have followed. But paths can become rutted. A couple who start their journey should make all of this their own, and should leave aside whatever seems sham and inauthentic. For instance, there was a custom for brides to walk over to the Mary-altar after Communion and leave their bouquets as a tribute to the Mother of Jesus. Nowadays if a bride troops over when everyone in the church knows it is her maiden voyage to a Lady Chapel, and she isn't going to leave her bouquet but only a cheap nosegay instead, the whole proceeding seems phony. If people simply comply with customs that have no sense for them, their wedding day can become a court ceremonial with the photographer leading them through the maneuvers.

Any great liturgical event is a gesture of disciplined passion: of routine that can burst into spontaneity. The Mass has a basic format that follows custom, but when it is best celebrated the community and its president put their mark on the rite, and would easily puzzle a stranger who had to guess what was traditional and what they had improvised. The people who succeed best at grasping the sense and feel of ancient routines in a Christian wedding will have the most authentic and tasteful creativity in adapting the rite to their own inspirations.

As at any Eucharist a wedding will include some readings from Scripture. Three readings are possible, with psalms or responsories in between. My own preference is for less—two readings or even one—so as to leave less jumble in the mind or memory. I would rather hear one substantially long reading that I can follow and dwell on afterward, than a succession of paragraphs scissored out of different biblical books. In any case, the person who is going to preach should indicate which reading(s) would most help him to frame his message. Many preachers will want to know the couple's own preferences among the roster of recommended Scripture texts, and will then shape the homily to them. There is hardly a better nourishment for pre-marital (or, for that matter, post-marital) meditation.

Catholics are perhaps the world's worst singers. Worst of all, at weddings when we should have most to sing about, we fall into an awful tradition of inappropriate hymns like *Ave Maria* and *Panis Angelicus* (since no one understands them they can't feel inappropriate), typically crooned or bawled from the balcony by a cousin of the groom. Then there was a violent swerve toward schlock ballads with ukelele-quality guitar continuo. If the congregation at a wedding is mostly composed of Catholics and is an assembly of worshipers that are strangers to one another, the *Titanic* could probably sink beneath them without a hymn. But if they do know one another, or if there is a good contingent of Protestants present, then with an encouraging celebrant and a compelling song leader and an adroit organist and some well-chosen hymns you ought to be able to sing at your wedding. And when better?

All too often people assemble stiffly in church for the "ritual" part of a wedding, and then unwind at a boisterous reception. Rightly celebrated, the mood should be the same at both. People should enjoy themselves with the same merriment in church that is going to enliven the reception afterward. And the reception, no less than the Mass, should be a happy event because a man and a woman have joined promises that defy death itself. When once you partake of this sort of wedding you understand how senseless it would be to invite anyone to one part of the festivities but not to the other.

A bachelor party the night before a wedding is usually a catastrophe. The spiritual character of this party in no way leads through into the spiritual character of the next day's events. If a marriage is scheduled for Saturday, the bachelor party should be not later than Thursday or not at all. Friday is reserved for the rehearsal dinner, which is a family-and-friends event. If the men have come to town only that day and want to enjoy each other's company at some length, and cannot be dissuaded from going out, there should be a clear understanding about an early hour to break it up. A wedding is a wonderful occasion for friends to gather, but the typical bachelor party seems out of character with the rest of the celebration.

No one seems to be able to get to a wedding rehearsal on time, but it is extremely inconvenient if they do not, for often there are other rehearsals scheduled immediately afterward. It is helpful to have the entire wedding party there, as well as the parents. The rehearsal is not just a practice session for the maneuvers of the ceremony. It is an inaugural event to enter into the mood of the wedding and of the marriage. It should be enjoyable in its own right. No one really needs to remember all that much, for the priest will lead people along the next day. But the rehearsal allows all to become familiar with what they will do, and able to move through it in a more personal way instead of like a military review.

The rehearsal dinner is usually an intimate time for the two families and their closest friends. I find it the perfect occasion for the bridal couple to stand up at the end of the meal and for both to tell their parents and grandparents of their gratitude for the love and service they have received over all the years. The wedding of a child is an extremely moving event in one's life, and amid all the bother and work and expense the rehearsal dinner offers a quiet time and select company for the things to be said which all too often go unsaid.

It is, of course, a tradition for the bridal party to dress festively and formally. All too often they dress uncomfortably. Brides should choose dresses that enhance them without inhibiting them. If the weather is going to be at all warm they should wear light material. Heavy eggshell satin with long sleeves and a high collar is a disaster in August. If a bride wishes to wear a train, well and good, provided that she can walk around with it following her by itself. She is going to wear this dress all day and needs to enjoy herself in it. If she spends her time worrying about wrinkles or soil or how it is arranged, she would be wiser to wear a floor-length dress. Many bridal dresses seem designed exclusively to be photographed from the rear while the bride is kneeling. Now that the Church is restoring the traditional postures at the Eucharist (sitting for readings and preaching; standing for the rest), it is less frequent for a bridal couple to be forced to kneel uncomfortably throughout their wedding. The dress should be a delight to wear, so much so that the bride will be reluctant to take it off at the end of the day. The groom and his party should never feel obliged to wear woolen formal clothes plus vest plus cummerbund plus starched shirt, if it is a wedding in high summer. They would do better to wear light, loose, soft fabrics. It is another sign of incongruity if the party is standing dressed to the nines before the altar, and then hours later has torn off jackets and ties and collars to be comfortable at the reception. As a rule the best dressed people at a wedding are the bridesmaids, who wear light, short-sleeved frocks. I don't know that groomsmen could imitate this, but they might learn from it.

It is a fine tradition for both bride and goom to exchange rings. Many like to engrave initials and the date of their wedding inside. There is now an increasing number of jewelers who make attractive wedding bands to order. America is one of the few places where an engagement ring is worn. The custom elsewhere is to wear a single wedding ring, but for that same ring to serve during engagement too. During that time it is worn on the other hand, and at the wedding it is then moved across to the wedding hand. This also allows the husband to have a token of his engagement.

There is a lovely English custom that the spouses exchange precious coins at their wedding. The formula for the exchange embodies the fullness of the marriage sharing:

With this ring I thee wed
this gold and silver I thee give
with my body I thee worship
and with all my worldly goods I thee endow.

Couples then often carry the coins as tokens of their wedding, on a bracelet or a watch fob.

It is enjoyable to have a good party of your closest friends stand up for you at your wedding, but sometimes the sanctuary looks like a mob scene. One custom in particular creates difficulties: ring-bearers and flower girls. These used to be close relatives, about ten to twelve years old. More recently the mean age for this role has descended to pre-school years, and these youngsters are often undone when the moment arrives to walk down the aisle. Or they distract everyone during the wedding because they have to be tended in the sanctuary. If they are really too young to feel the honor of being included, they are too young to be of help.

One of the options which has recently become available affects the manner in which the wedding party enters the church. The ushers should previously have set the tone by welcoming guests and leading them down the aisle with the tangible sense that they are arriving for a celebration that is awesome and enjoyable. They are welcoming people to a party, and should not walk stiffly like pallbearers at a military burial. The great entry is of the wedding party itself, and everyone is familiar with the traditional mode wherein the groom and his men enter from the front and await the bride with her companions and her father. An alternative is for the entire party to enter in the same way. The celebrant and his party lead the way down the aisle, followed by the groomsmen who lead in the groom with his parents on either arm, followed by the bride with her party and both parents. Some find this less redolent of an age when women were so subordinated that they could not make formal public appearances except with a male escort. And it allows both families to bring their own child and offer a strong symbolic support to the union.

The reader or readers should be chosen less with an eye to honoring some relative than with an ear to having everyone hear the word clearly and loudly.

In an older style of doing things, at the crest of the wedding ceremony the couple would be huddled with the priest, turning their backs to the rest of the gathering and murmuring inaudibly. Since everyone in the church is there to witness these vows, it is much more appropriate if the wedding party gathers in a semicircle that faces the congregation. The presiding celebrant can then stand down the steps, in the vicinity of the parents, and address them as the leader of the assembly, and call for them to state themselves audibly and forthrightly. It is better still if the couple have learned their vows by heart, so that they can say them personally to one another, instead of reciting them phrase-by-phrase after they are dictated by the priest.

Just before the vows themselves it is fitting for the priest to turn to each of the families present and ask them publicly if they are willing to accept into their midst this new daughter or grandson or sister, and to give them the love and support they would give their own kin.

It is very difficult for married couples to attend a wedding and not feel their own promises aroused all over again. If they are not on good terms at the time it can be painful. But if they are, they sense themselves drawn in especially at the moment of the pledging. It can be very helpful to them if the celebrant invites them at that moment, if they are sitting beside one another, to rejoin hands in memory of these same promises made in days past and kept long since.

At the kiss of peace it is right for everyone in the church to have more time than usual to greet one another. It is certainly as good a time as at the reception for the exchanges that a wedding seems to call for. The bridal couple especially should go to greet their parents: each of them has the old family that brought him or her to that day, and a new family that has just made room for her or him in their midst. These must all be hugged and kissed. Let it all go on as long as it will.

At the end of the rite, when the blessings are to be given, it is good to reassemble the wedding party facing the people, as it was for the exchange of vows. Then the parents are grateful to be invited to enter the sanctuary and stand behind the couple and put their hands on their shoulders so as to join the priest when he blesses them. Parents want to bless their children, old and new, and it is the service of the Church to invite them to do it at such a high moment.

At the very end, as the wedding party is retiring, I favor another English custom whereby the father of the groom offers his arm to the mother of the bride to escort her out, and vice versa (the same with all family members, if you wish): this embodies the union between the two families which the wedding has just established.

These are only a few things said by way of suggestion. Read over the rite well together, and go to a few weddings in the meantime. It will stir up your sense of how you would best like to celebrate the day that will rise up in your memory many days later.

# *Appendix*
## *Address to the Bride and Groom*

My dear friends: you are about to enter into a union which is most sacred and most serious. It is most sacred, because established by God himself; most serious, because it will bind you together for life in a relationship so close and so intimate, that it will profoundly affect your whole future. That future, with its hopes and disappointments, its successes and its failures, its pleasures and its pains, its joys and its sorrows, is now hidden from your eyes: yet you know that these elements are part of every life and should be expected in your own. And so, not knowing what is before you, you take each other for better or for worse, for richer or for poorer, in sickness and in health, until death.

Truly, then, these words are most serious. It is a beautiful tribute to your undoubted faith in each other that, recognizing their full import, you are nevertheless so willing and ready to pronounce them. And because these words involve such solemn obligations, it is most fitting that you rest the security of your wedded life upon the great principle of self-sacrifice. And so you begin your married life with the voluntary and complete surrender of your individual lives in the interest of that deeper and wider life which you are to have in common. Henceforth you belong entirely to each other: you will be one in mind, one in heart, and one in affections. And whatever sacrifices you may hereafter be required to make for the preservation of this mutual life, always make them generously. Sacrifice is usually difficult and irksome. Only love can make it easy; and perfect love can make it a joy. We are willing to give in proportion as we love. And when love is perfect, the sacrifice is complete. God so loved the world that he gave his only begotten Son; and the Son so loved us that he gave himself for our salvation. Greater love than this no one has, than to lay down one's life for one's friends.

No greater blessing can come upon your married life than pure conjugal love, loyal and true to the end. May, then, this love with which you join your hands and hearts today, never fail, but grow deeper and stronger as the years go on. And if true love and the unselfish spirit of perfect sacrifice guide your every action, you can expect the greatest measure of earthly happiness that may be allotted to humans in this vale of tears. The rest is in the hands of God. Nor will God be wanting to your needs: he will pledge you the lifelong support of his graces in the holy sacrament you are now going to receive.

*(This address to the marrying couple originated in the United States, where it formed a regular part of the Catholic wedding rite until recently. It remains one of the finest liturgical texts in the English language.)*

**Also by James Tunstead Burtchaell from other publishers:**

**Catholic Theories of Biblical Inspiration since 1810: A Review and Critique** (Cambridge University Press, 1969)

**Philemon's Problem: The Daily Dilemma of the Christian** (ACTA, 1973)

**Marriage Among Christians: A Curious Tradition** (Ave Maria, 1977) [editor]

**Bread and Salt: A Cassette Catechism** (NCR Credence Cassettes, 1978)

**Abortion Parley** (Andrews & McMeel, 1980) [editor]

**Rachel Weeping, and Other Essays on Abortion** (Andrews & McMeel, 1982; Harper & Row [paperback], 1984) Christopher Prize, 1982

# DATE DUE